101 Places You Gotta See Before You're 12!

4/07

101 Places You Gotta See Before You're 12!

Joanne O'Sullivan

Louisburg Library
Bringing People and Information Together

A Division of Sterling Publishing Co., Inc.
New York

Creative Director:
Celia Naranjo

Designer:
Robin Gregory

Cover Photograph:
© Birgid Allig/Taxi/Getty Images

Art Production Assistant:
Bradley Norris

Editorial Assistant:
Rose McLarney

Editorial Assistance:
Susan Kieffer
Delores Gosnell
Dawn Dillingham
Rosemary Kast

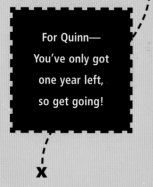

For Quinn—
You've only got
one year left,
so get going!

Library of Congress Cataloging-in-Publication Data

O'Sullivan, Joanne.
  101 places you gotta see before you're 12 / by Joanne O'Sullivan.— 1st ed.
      p. cm.
  Includes index.
  ISBN 1-57990-865-9 (pbk.)
  1. Travel—Guidebooks. I. Title. II. Title: One hundred one places you gotta see before you're twelve.
G153.4.O88 2006
910.4—dc22

                          2006001622

10 9 8 7 6 5 4 3 2

Published by Lark Books, A Division of
Sterling Publishing Co., Inc.
387 Park Avenue South, New York, N.Y. 10016

© 2006, Lark Books

Distributed in Canada by Sterling Publishing, c/o Canadian Manda Group, 165 Dufferin Street, Toronto, Ontario, Canada M6K 3H6

Distributed in the United Kingdom by GMC Distribution Services, Castle Place, 166 High Street, Lewes, East Sussex, England BN7 1XU

Distributed in Australia by Capricorn Link (Australia) Pty Ltd., P.O. Box 704, Windsor, NSW 2756 Australia

If you have questions or comments about this book, please contact:
Lark Books, 67 Broadway, Asheville, NC 28801
(828) 253-0467

Manufactured in China

ISBN 13: 978-1-57990-865-2
ISBN 10: 1-57990-865-9

For information about custom editions, special sales, premium and corporate purchases, please contact Sterling Special Sales Department at 800-805-5489 or specialsales@sterlingpub.com.

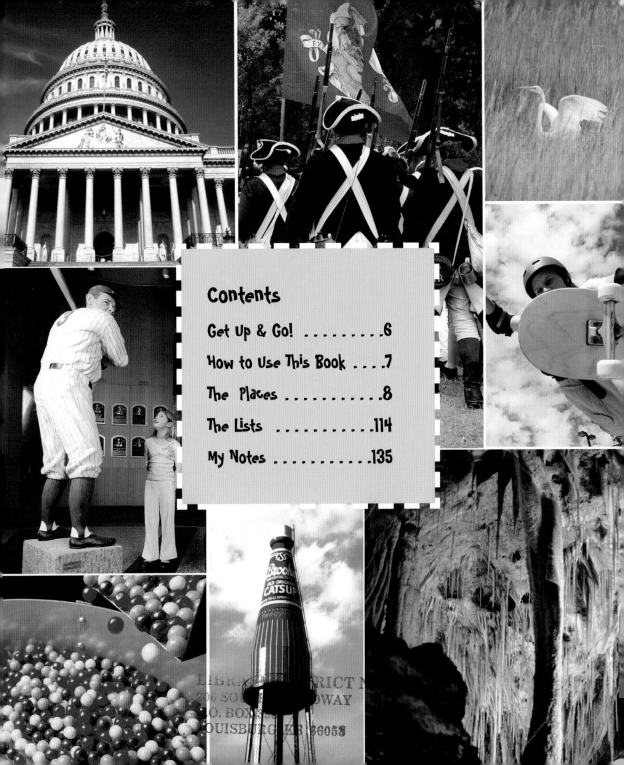

Contents

Get Up & Go! x

LONG AGO, THE EARLY EXPLORERS SET OFF ON THEIR JOURNEYS with nothing more than a spirit of adventure and the stars to guide them. Sometimes the only information they had about their destination was an ominous phrase written on the edge of a map: *Here there be dragons.* Today, we have global positioning satellites to tell us where we are all the time, and guidebooks that tell us exactly what we *should* see and *will* see when we get to a certain place at a certain time. True, people don't get lost in jungles or eaten by sea monsters much these days, but sometimes, having too much information can make exploring a little less exciting.

That's where this book comes in. It isn't a book, really. It's more like a scavenger hunt. Instead of hunting for *things,* you'll be hunting for cool places and amazing experiences. How will you find them? We'll give you some clues: a list of 101 places, a reference guide for finding them, stickers to rate and keep track of them, a map, a journal section for your notes, and a pocket for your souvenirs. The rest is up to you. No two kids are exactly the same, so no two journeys will be the same—which makes your discoveries truly your own. You may not live in the Age of Explorers, but you're definitely the right age for exploring. Before you're 12 is the perfect time to get out and see the world.

How to Use This Book   x

- Read through the list of 101 places. From old-growth forests to archeological sites, haunted houses to skateparks, landfills to famous ball fields—there's a huge variety of places to see, both near your neighborhood and far away. The best thing about these 101 places, though, is that there are actually *way* more than 101 of them. For each kind of place, there could be five, 10, or even 100 specific examples for you to see all over North America. (There are 124 lighthouses in the state of Michigan alone!) *You* choose!

- Figure out which places you've already seen and which ones you want to go to next. Use the **stickers** to keep track of where you want to go and where you've been. Rate the ones you liked or didn't like and even create your own Top 20 Places list. Each entry has a **spiral squiggle** where you can place a sticker. (Of course you can put your stickers wherever you want.)

Put your sticker here

- Use **The Lists** beginning on page 114 and the **map** inside the back cover to help you start exploring. Find out which places are near where you live, where you're going on vacation, or where you have extended family. Plan a road trip with your family. Convince a teacher to organize a field trip to one (or more!) of the places in this book. Some places are so close by, you might even be able to stop by a few on your way home from school. See as many places as you can! (The U.S. states and Canadian provinces, along with their abbreviations, are also on page 114.)

- Save some mementos of your excursions and trips—photos, postcards, tickets, etc.— and keep them in **the pocket** at the front of the book.

- Keep a record of the places you've visited and notes about your exploring on the **My Notes** pages beginning on page 135. Write down addresses, thoughts, opinions, or memories (use a pen or a thin, permanent marker so you don't smudge).

So, what's your reward at the end of this scavenger hunt? A collection of incredible experiences, a lot of fun new discoveries, amazing memories, and a lot of great stories to tell your friends. Even if you don't see all these places before you're 12, you'll have made a great start to a lifetime of exploration.

There's nothing like the thrill of discovering new places. Along the way you might just make some unexpected discoveries about yourself, too. And believe it or not, there are still some places where you might get to see sea monsters (see page 45). *Bon Voyage!*

1. A Lighthouse

Imagine the things a lighthouse has seen: clipper ships in full sail, battles at sea, and maybe even pirates—things we'll never see. Visiting a lighthouse is like traveling back in time, to the era before cars and airplanes, when crossing the ocean took months, not hours, and a light shining on the shore in the night could mean the difference between life and death for a sailor. Besides all that, lighthouses happen to be located in some of the most amazing places, and some will let you climb (hundreds of steps) to the top for a view you'll never forget.

Which state has the most lighthouses? It's Michigan, with around 124 lighthouses still standing.

Daymarks & Characteristics

From out at sea, one lighthouse could look pretty much like the next. That's why lighthouse keepers created a system to distinguish one from another.

Daymarks are the patterns painted on the towers that can be seen during daylight hours (see photos). *Characteristics* are the light patterns that are flashed at night. These patterns help sea captains map their position along the coast. Here are some examples:

Block Island North, Rhode Island:
One white flash every five seconds

Block Island South, Rhode Island:
One green flash every five seconds

Pigeon Point, California:
One flash every ten seconds

Assateague, Virginia:
Double flash every five seconds

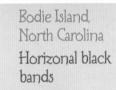

Bodie Island, North Carolina
Horizonal black bands

Cape Hatteras, North Carolina
Black swirling bands

West Quoddy, Maine
Horizontal red bands

Check out the list of lighthouses on page 115 to find one near you, or go to **www.unc.edu/rowlett/lighthouse** for a directory of lighthouses in North America.

2. A LANDFILL

What weighs as much as a rhinoceros and never disappears? Give up? It's the amount of garbage you *personally* generate every year: 4 pounds a day, every day. Combine that with garbage created by everyone else in the country, and you've got 210 million tons of trash—enough to cover the entire state of Rhode Island, 6 feet deep. So where does it all go? Most of it ends up in a landfill, and you should make a point to visit it. It may not be the prettiest (or most fragrant place) you'll see in your travels, but when you see it, it will really hit you: *Hey, I need to recycle!*

To find out the location of your local landfill and how to visit, look in the phone directory for your county or municipal waste management office.

The highest point in Ohio is said to be Mount Rumpke—a mountain made of trash (a landfill!).

3. An Artist's Studio

This is where the magic happens: fire and sand are transformed into glass, globs of clay are molded into fantastic sculptures, and paint and brushes make a canvas come alive. An artist's studio is a place where imagination can run free and the only rule is that there are no rules. No two artists are alike, so no two studios are the same either. You might see a paint-splattered space with soaring ceilings or a cozy cottage outfitted with a potter's wheel and a kiln. But you need to visit an artist's studio to see how many different ways there are to express yourself and get your own creative juices flowing.

Check your phone book to find your local Arts Council, and then call for information on which artists offer studio visits, or check your newspaper for studio tour announcements.

Snow geese in flight over Sandhill cranes in Nebraska

4. A Migration Path

It's kind of like an invisible superhighway for animals. No one knows how they know when to start and where to go, but millions of animals return all together to these paths at the same time every year as they journey from their winter to summer homes and back again. If you're in the right place at the right time, in one day you can see more birds, butterflies, bats, frogs, and even snakes than you've ever seen in your whole life! The animals load up on food, conduct elaborate mating rituals, make big piles of *guano*, then go on their way. Being outnumbered by animals 10,000 to one is an awesome experience!

Sandhill Cranes
Where: Platte River, NE
When: Late February, for six weeks
How many: Half a million!
Crane Meadows Nature Center
www.cranemeadows.org

Stinkpot Turtles, Leopard Frogs, and other amphibians
Where: Shawnee Nat'l. Forest, IL
When: March, September (Sunny days in the fall are said to be best)
How many: Hundreds of some, thousands of others
www.fs.fed.us/r9/forests/shawnee

Mexican Free-Tailed Bats
Where: Texas Hill Country
When: April and May
How many: 20 million
Bracken Bat Cave
North of San Antonio, TX
www.batcon.org/discover/bracken.html

Monarch Butterflies
Where: Pacific Grove, CA
When: Early October
How many: About 25,000
Monarch Grove Sanctuary
www.ci.pg.ca.us/monarchs/

Manatees
Where: Crystal River, FL
When: November - March
How many: Hundreds
Crystal River National Wildlife Refuge
www.fws.gov/crystalriver

Stellar Sea Lions
Where: Sea Lion Caves, near Florence, OR
When: All year, but June-August is breeding season
How many: Hundreds
www.sealioncaves.com

Garter Snakes
Where: Narcisse, MB
When: September, April/May
How many: About 20,000
www.gov.mb.ca, search 'Narcisse'

Birds, Birds, Birds!
Where: Point Pelee National Park, ON, and Cape May Point Park, NJ
When: April-May (also fall at Cape May)
How many: More than 400 varieties of birds
www.pc.gc.ca, search 'Point Pelee'

Cape May Point Park, NJ
www.state.nj.us/dep/parksandforests
search 'Cape May'

5. A Skatepark

To find a skatepark near you, call your local parks and recreation department, or search for one on: **www.skateboard parks.com**.

NO SKATEBOARDS ALLOWED: You see the signs everywhere. But there's a place where skaters aren't just allowed, they *rule*: a skatepark. Instead of grass, paths, and trees, in this kind of park, you'll find concrete ramps and other features designed to let skaters do what they do best: defy gravity, hang in midair, leap over obstacles, and even do flips, all without ever dropping their boards. Even if you don't know a quarter pipe from a snake run, or a combi-bowl from a flow section, you should see a skatepark. Go on a day when there's a competition for a really cool experience.

6. A Working Farm

Before you take a bite of that seemingly healthy breakfast bar, look at the side of the box and read the ingredients: artificial colors and flavors, 25-letter words you've never heard of…What is that stuff? Where does it come from? At this point, you should remember a simple rule: the closer your food is to where it came from, the better it is for you. That's why you need to visit a farm. At a farm you can trace your food's journey from planting to harvesting and out into the world. You'll learn what's in season when (and hopefully take some of the freshest picks home with you), and maybe even get to collect some eggs or milk a cow—you can't get much closer to your food than that!

Call your County Extension Agent to find out which farms in your area are open for public visits.

7. A Space Place

FOUR, THREE, TWO, ONE—BLAST OFF!
Experience 'g-force acceleration,' feel what a
blastoff is like, sit inside a rocket, see pictures
of the sun's surface, and get a taste of life on
Mars. You can do all this and more at a space
center or museum. Space exploration is an amazing combination of science and imagination—the
perfect example of what people mean when they
say "if you can dream it, you can do it." Scientists
and engineers have made it possible to go places
and see things that no one would have
thought possible just a generation ago.
Start dreaming now, and who knows
how far you can go...

What does it
feel like to be inside a rocket
launching into outer space? Find
out for yourself at the
U.S. Space and Rocket
Center in Huntsville,
Alabama (see page 115
for more info).

8. An Animal Rescue Center

From oil spills to predator attacks or mean owners, animals face a lot of dangers in the world. Just like people, they need a safe place they can go for food, shelter, and the care they deserve. Animal sanctuaries, refuges, and rescue centers are those kinds of places. They take in injured wild animals, treat, and release them, or give orphaned, abused, and neglected animals a happy home.

S.O.S. — Save our seals! See them (and whales, dolphins, and sea otters) at the Marine Mammal Center, Sausalito, CA.

There are cats, and then there are big cats—see them at Big Cat Rescue, Tampa, FL.

Elephants find a safe haven at The Elephant Sanctuary, Hohenwald, TN.

If you can't get to a wild animal rescue center, check out a local shelter for dogs and cats. Call your local Society for the Protection of Animals (SPCA) for more information.

Some animal sanctuaries specialize in certain kinds of animals, while others will take any animal in need. If you're an animal lover, you've gotta meet the people who make the world a safer place for animals, and you've gotta give their animals a little more love!

9. A Superlative Place

Mount McKinley, the highest peak in the U.S.

In case you were absent the day superlatives were discussed in language arts class, a superlative is an adjective that's used to compare things. Superlatives usually end in *est*: highest, longest, smallest, deepest, or most (rather than *mest*—English doesn't always make sense, does it?). A superlative place is the most something place in the country or maybe the world. Why see one? Because it's a kind of measuring stick against which to judge all other places. And it will impress your friends when you say, "Yes, this mountain is tall, but I've seen the tallest one in the whole country." You might want to make up some of your own superlatives, too: "That is the *ugliest* house I've ever seen."

TALLEST TREES IN THE UNITED STATES AND CANADA

Humboldt Redwoods State Park, Weott, CA

The Carmanah Giant, Carmanah Walbran Provincial Park Vancouver Island, BC

TALLEST MOUNTAIN IN THE U.S., "LOWER 48," AND CANADA

Mt. McKinley, AK   20, 320 feet (17 of the 20 tallest peaks in the U.S. are in Alaska)

Mt. Whitney, CA   14, 494 feet

Mt. Logan, YT   19,551 feet

OLDEST BASEBALL STADIUM

Fenway Park, Boston, MA

WORLD'S LONGEST SUBWAY

New York, NY: 468 stations

BIGGEST CANYON IN NORTH AMERICA (right)

The Grand Canyon (of course): 277 miles long

WORLD'S LARGEST LIBRARY
Library of Congress (below)

Washington, DC: 130 million items on 530 miles of bookshelves

BIGGEST LAKE IN NORTH AMERICA (above)

Lake Superior: 31,700 square miles

THE WORLD'S SMALLEST DESERT

Carcross Desert, near Carcross, YT 260 hectares (about 642 acres)

COLDEST PLACE IN NORTH AMERICA

Snag, YT (had the coldest recorded temperature at -81°F)

OLDEST EUROPEAN SETTLEMENT IN NORTH AMERICA

St. Augustine, FL, or St. John's, NL

LONGEST RIVER IN THE U.S. AND CANADA

Missouri   2,540 miles

Mackenzie   2,629 miles

LONGEST HIGHWAY IN THE WORLD

Trans-Canada Highway: 4,860 miles

DEATH VALLEY, CALIFORNIA IS A TRIPLE SUPERLATIVE— it's one of the hottest places on the planet, it's 282 feet below sea level (making it the lowest), and it's also the driest place in North America.

The most faraway island in the world is Bouvet Island, the most remote spot on Earth. Its closest neighbor is another remote island more than 1,000 miles away.

10. A Faraway Island

If you had been born in the Age of Explorers, you could have just gotten into a boat, "discovered" a new land, and named it after you (Isle de Sam—sounds pretty good, doesn't it?). But even though most places have been discovered, they still need to be explored. Find an island— in the ocean, in a lake, or even in a river—the harder an island is to get to, the better it will be when you get there. No bridges to the mainland, preferably no cars, and even better, no people! Once you get to your island, you will be rewarded for your perseverance: and if it's a sea island, you'll get the best pick of the shells because there will be no competition. And even though it already has a name on the map, you can rename it after you, your dog, or anything else you come up with.

11. An Antiquarian Bookstore

A good used or antiquarian bookstore is a place where you can spend hours rooting around and never know the time has passed. Pick up any book from the shelf that looks interesting, and you're off on a time-travel adventure—look at the pictures of the funny way people used to dress; read a few lines and see how differently people used to think and write. See old maps that chart countries that don't exist anymore, or read old predictions about what life would be like in the future (we were supposed to be living on Mars by now?!). Some antiquarian bookstores even have books that are hundreds of years old that they'll let you look at (very carefully). And (unlike a library) if you find something really special, you can take it home to keep. Use your local phone directory to find a store near you.

12. An Old-Growth Forest

The first European settlers arrived in North America to find towering trees covering the land. But they needed open fields for farming and wood for houses and warmth, so down went the trees—almost all of them. Luckily, they missed a few spots, and these places, called old-growth forests, are full of ancient trees (think *ents* from *The Lord of the Rings*). Stand under a tree as tall as a 20-story building: you can see what the forests must have looked like in the past and you'll understand what the word *majestic* means. It's truly an awesome experience that you just gotta have.

13. A Ghost Town

Main Street, Bodie, California

The ghost of a mine in Montana

For information on ghost towns in every state and province, go to **www.ghosttowns.com**.

A Texas ghost town, formerly known as Neches

The mill shut down. The train stopped coming. There was a big flood. There are lots of reasons a town can become a ghost town—left with nothing but empty, abandoned houses, stores, and churches. Gold rush towns in the West are some of the best-known, but there are ghost towns in every state and province. Although some are falling to pieces, some remain much the way they were when the last residents moved away. Visiting a ghost town gives you a strange feeling—not really scary, but eerie and a little unsettling, and kind of exciting. Go see one and find out for yourself.

14. A Waterfall

Unless you happen to be accidentally going over one in a runaway raft, a waterfall is incredibly peaceful and inviting. There's nothing like the sound of the rushing water: even before you see the waterfall, you can hear it from a distance, calling you to come closer. The misty spray from the falls feels deliciously cool on your skin (especially after the hike you took to get there), and the amazing sight of thousands of gallons of water tumbling over rocks takes your breath away. And believe it or not, waterfalls even have their own smell—a kind of deep, earthy, watery scent. A waterfall is a delightful experience for all your senses.

15. An Olympic Training Center

The Olympic Games are the ultimate event for any athlete—the chance to compete against the best in the world, break records, win medals, or achieve a personal best. You may not be able to attend the actual games, but you can watch the world's fastest, strongest, and best athletes preparing for them at an Olympic Training Center. Catch a trial or qualifying event, or just watch as athletes go through their daily training routines. You'll see first-hand that being a world-class athlete requires more than natural talent. Behind every perfect dive or dismount, there's a lot of frustration and hard work. That's why Olympic athletes are so inspiring and you gotta see them do their thing.

For information about Olympic trials and qualifying events held in different locations, go to **www.olympic-usa.org** for the U.S. Olympic Committee or **www.olympic.ca/EN/index.shtml** for the Canadian Olympic Committee.

16. A Swimming Hole

Deep in the woods or under a desert cliff, there's a watery place: smaller than a lake, wider than a creek, deeper than a puddle. It's surrounded by rocks or trees and maybe even a waterfall. It's called a swimming hole, and it's for swimming the way it was meant to be. The best swimming holes are usually found by word of mouth, and some of them are closely guarded secrets. You may have to bribe someone for directions. But you'll be glad you did. Once there, you can splash and be as loud as you want: there are no rules at a swimming hole.

Top Five Reasons to Swim in a Swimming Hole

5. Your hair won't turn green from the chlorine

4. You'll be sharing the water with fish

3. There's adventure and surprise— what *was* that thing that just brushed up against me?

2. No concrete scrapes on your feet

1. No adult swim!

Caution: Always swim with a buddy, don't dive into water if you don't know the water's depth, and watch out for fast-moving currents.

Check the map on **www.swimmingholes.org** to see whether you can find some good swimming holes near you.

17. A Kooky Capital

Quick—name the capital of Wyoming! If you guessed Cheyenne, you were right. But what about the sock capital of the world—bet you don't know that one. Still thinking? It's Fort Payne, Alabama, where one in every four socks in the United States is made. Lots of towns have made claims to be the world capital of something or other. Visit a kooky capital near you and see whether it lives up to its claim.

See polar bears in their natural habitat at the Polar Bear Capital of the World, Churchill, Manitoba.

See what the buzz is about in Hidalgo, Texas, the Killer Bee Capital of the World.

Trolls rule in Mount Horeb, Wisconsin, the Troll Capital of the World.

Art can take you places you've never been—to faraway countries, imaginary worlds, the ancient past, or even to a feeling. That's why a visit to an art museum is like going to a million different places at once: a park in Paris, circa 1900; the streets of Florence during the Renaissance; a mountaintop in China, centuries ago. Art takes you there. Sometimes an art museum can make you nervous or overwhelmed—there's so much to see, and some art you just don't *get*. That's okay. Nobody likes everything in a museum, and sometimes the "great" art just doesn't do it for you. But keep an open mind, and somewhere you're sure to find something that takes you someplace you've always wanted to go.

Suits of armor are works of art, too.

The big kahuna of art museums—
The Metropolitan Museum of Art in New York City

The Swineherd, Brittany, by Paul Gaugin,
Los Angeles County Museum of Art

19. A Rock Art Site ◎

It's not a place for CD cover art—it's a place where you can find 5,000-year-old engravings and paintings, just *sitting* right there on the rocks! No tickets, no glass cases—just *petroglyphs* (engravings on stone) and *pictographs* (paintings on stone), some from the time of the last Ice Age. These images of people, bison, mountain lions, coyotes, and other animals have survived (in the wind, rain, and snow for thousands of years) even though the people who created them have disappeared, leaving no other trace of their culture. Wouldn't it be cool to make something that lasted that long?

Nine Mile Canyon, Utah, called "the world's longest art gallery," is home to more than 10,000 rock art symbols and images.

20. A Wind Farm

So, you're riding along the highway, just looking out at a whole lot of nothing, when all of a sudden, what's that in that field over there? An army of colossal three-armed alien droids assembled, ready take over and destroy the earth? No, it's a wind farm! And it looks like nothing you've ever seen: massive turbines on towers more than 200 feet tall, whirring slowly or quickly in the wind, dominating the landscape like giants. They're strangely beautiful, like modern art sculptures, and they make a gentle swooshing sound while they transform wind into electricity without the use of air-polluting coal. But wind farms don't just look really cool: take a tour of one and find out how they may just *save* the planet.

21. An Aquarium

It's really exciting to see a shark up close, but it's also nice to have a few feet of reinforced glass between you when you do. Aquariums let you observe all kinds of cool underwater creatures that usually speed away when humans come near, or, in the case of sharks, that make *humans* speed away. You can see rare tropical fish and sea anemones that only scuba divers usually get to see, and some aquariums even have adorable sea mammals such as dolphins, sea otters, seals, or manatees. Watching all the creatures dive, float, flit, and flock through clear blue water in graceful motions almost puts you into a trance until: snap! It's feeding time and the shark opens up those big jaws for a bite to eat, reminding you that under the sea everybody is somebody else's lunch!

22. A "Little" Country

North America is often called a melting pot—everyone who comes here brings a little flavor of his or her own culture to the mix. Sample one of these fascinating flavors when you visit a place where immigrants keep their cultural traditions alive. Walk down the bustling streets of a Chinatown, and you'll hear people speaking in dozens of dialects and see storefronts filled with intriguing items. Eat a steamy hot bowl of pho at a restaurant in a Little Saigon. Check out the Indian hip-hop CDs and beautiful sari fabrics in the stores of a Little India. Listen to the Muslim call to prayers in a Middle Eastern neighborhood. There are so many amazing experiences to be had in a "little city" near you—no passport required.

23. A Crazy Dream House

Scotty's Castle
Walter Scott couldn't find gold in Death Valley, but he did find a rich investor to help him build a 'castle' there. Scotty's Castle features many wonders, including a huge theater organ and an indoor waterfall.

For some people a house is just a place to live. For others it's an expression of personal creativity. An ordinary dwelling just won't do—they'll settle for nothing less than a castle. While lots of these imaginative houses are off-limits, many are open to the public so you can get a peak at a famously fantastic home. It's fun to see the cool and crazy ideas people come up with for their dream homes—indoor waterfalls and carousels, personal theaters, grand banquet halls—the sky's the limit. After you see one of these out-of-this-world dream homes, you may just want to go home and give your room a makeover.

Gillette Castle
He made millions as one of the most famous actors of his time. Then William Gillette built his spectacular home in East Haddam, Connecticut based on a Norman castle.

A seven-story house with stairs leading to the ceiling, doors leading nowhere, and closest doors that open to brick walls—The Winchester Mystery House in San Jose, California is not only strange, it's said to be haunted.

24. The House Where Your Parent(s) Grew Up

"It used to be so much bigger" is probably the first thing your mom or dad will say. Your dad will start to tell you lots of funny stories about what he used to do and the time he got in so much trouble for something he would never let you do. Your mom will talk about trees or bushes that used to be there, or who her neighbors were, or she'll start digging in the yard for something she buried long ago. She might even start to cry. You may learn more about your parent from this one visit than you've ever known. And you may find out that underneath all that grown-up stuff, your parent is really a kid at heart.

25. A Famous Field

You've probably seen it a million times on TV while you're watching the game or match. But when you see it in person for the first time, it'll give you goosebumps. It's so *big*. And so many unforgettable sports moments have happened here, bringing the crowd to its feet and filling the space with the deafening roar of cheers. Go on a game day and you'll feel the electric atmosphere of excitement, or, if possible, go on a behind-the-scenes tour, and see the locker rooms, press rooms, and dugout. You can look at the field, or court, or rink, and dream of playing there one day. Can't you just hear the crowd chanting your name?

Yankee Stadium in Bronx, New York, home of the world-famous New York Yankees

26. A BIG CAVE

Caves have kind of a bad reputation. In books and movies, they're often the place where scary things (or people!) are hiding: creepy bats, mean grizzly bears, ghosts, fugitives from the law, etc. But to see the other side of the story, you really have to go to a cave—a really big, world-class cave. Underground lakes, rivers, waterfalls, walls made of crystal, chambers the size of football fields: you can find all of this in caves, plus a few bats, too.

With more than 360 miles of mapped caves, Mammoth Cave in Mammoth Cave, Kentucky is the world's longest recorded cave system.

KNOW YOUR ITES!

Stalactite: An icicle-shaped mineral deposit that hangs down from the roof of a cave or cavern (see below).

Stalagmite: Same shape, but this kind of deposit comes up from the floor of a cave (see left).

Calcite: The stuff that stalactites and stalagmites are made of (a type of mineral formation).

Anthodite: These formations look like little sea anemones made out of crystals, but, geologically speaking, they're a type of speleothem (mineral deposit) (see left, below).

Helictite: Sometimes described as looking like curly fries or clumps of worms, they're a rare and beautiful type of speleothem.

To find a cave near you, go to the National Caves Association website at **http://cavern.com**.

27. A Geyser or Natural Hot Springs

We all need to let off some steam every once in a while, and planet Earth is no exception. When things get too hot to handle down under the Earth's surface, it's time for a little geothermal activity. Sometimes earth shoots out steam all fast and furious (it's called a geyser); sometimes it heats up water below the surface slowly, which emerges in springs and pools, called hot springs. Some hot springs are so steaming, bubbling hot they're dangerous to touch, but others are deliciously warm, inviting you to take a dip. There are thousands of hot springs (and a couple of dozen geysers) in North America, most in places where there's been volcanic activity in the past. Visit one to see how cool it is to be hot.

Riverside Geyser in Yellowstone National Park erupts for 20 minutes every six hours or so.

28. Your Elected Official's Office

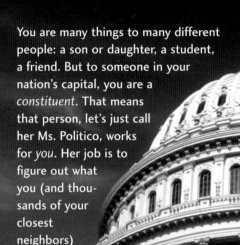

You are many things to many different people: a son or daughter, a student, a friend. But to someone in your nation's capital, you are a *constituent*. That means that person, let's just call her Ms. Politico, works for *you*. Her job is to figure out what you (and thousands of your closest neighbors) think about certain issues, and how she can represent your views. So you need to tell her what you think. That's right, little old you can schedule a meeting with her (or one of her staff members), and let your views be known. She may not always agree with your opinion, but she is professionally obligated to listen to you! Isn't democracy cool?

Here's how you can visit:

For the U.S.
Go to **www.congress.gov**. Click on "House Directory" or "Senate Directory."
Look up members by their name or by your state.

For Canada
Go to **www.parl.gc.ca/common/senmemb/senate/isenator.asp?Language=E**.
Find the member's name, then click on his or her profile to find the email address.

An insectarium can be a very noisy place. It's not the buzzing of the bees or the clicking of the beetles that makes it loud—it's the squeals and screams and shrieks of your fellow insectarium-goers as they watch hairy-legged tarantulas crawling nearby or cockroaches scuttling around a pretend kitchen looking for food.

See rare bugs, up close and personal.

29. An Insectarium

Try Szechuan scorpions at an 'Insect Tasting' at the Montreal Insectarium.

Explore the world of ants, flies, spiders, bees, "walking sticks," and butterflies without having to worry about bites, stings, or weird icky secretions getting on you. It's cool and creepy all at the same time. Some insectariums even host bug-tasting events—sweet or spicy bugs prepared by famous chefs. Can't you just hear the shrieking already?

Find out where the expression 'bug-eyed' comes from.

30. A Marvel of Engineering

They said it was impossible; they said it couldn't be done. But somewhere, a group of engineers believed that the bridge could span the bay, the tunnel could cut through the mountains, the tower could stretch higher into the sky. Everywhere we look, there are structures that help us surmount natural obstacles, get us where we want to go faster and more safely, or simply defy our expectations about what is possible. Some look so amazing, you can't believe that they don't just crumble or tumble down. But they won't! That's what makes them so "marvelous" and why you just gotta see them.

The Golden Gate Bridge, San Francisco, California

31. A Cemetery

When it comes to cemeteries, there are basically two types of people: those who find them scary, creepy, or boring, and those who find them endlessly interesting. If you are in the second category, you don't need any convincing to go to a cemetery—you've probably already gone. If you are in the first group, here are a few reasons to change your mind. Cemeteries are only scary or creepy if you go at night, which is illegal anyway. Cemeteries are *not* boring. The names on the headstones alone are worth going for—when was the last time you met someone named Epaphroditus or Sophronia? Then there's the cause of death—cholera, diptheria—diseases doctors found cures for. From cool crypts to interesting epitaths, you'll learn a lot about history. Just give it a try— you don't have to *stay* there.

32. A Wildlife Refuge

If you live in the city or the suburbs, the closest you probably get to seeing wildlife on a daily basis is watching the squirrels in your yard or the pigeons in the park. Nothing against squirrels, but if you want to have a *really cool* wildlife experience, you gotta go to a wildlife refuge. You can see wild ponies, buffalos, elk, or alligators in their natural habitat, with no cages or bars to hold them in. You might hear an elk "bugle" (a crazy-sounding mating call), watch big horn sheep lock horns, or see baby pelicans being born. It's awesome to observe animals on their own turf, and it sure beats pigeon watching (nothing against pigeons, of course).

To find more refuges in your area, go to **www.fws.gov/refuges** for the United States or **www.pc.gc.ca** for Canada.

Where the buffalo roam—The National Bison Range, Moiese, Montana

In the winter months, you can see nearly 8,000 elk at the National Elk Refuge, Jackson, Wyoming.

33. A LONG TRAIL

You may never choose to hike all the way from Canada to Mexico, but isn't it great to know that you could if you wanted to? The "long trails," as they're called, take you through some of the world's most amazing places: along the tops of mountain ranges, into wild forests, past crater lakes. You could hike a whole trail. But, of course, you'd have to take a year or so off from school (this is sounding better and better, isn't it?). Start with a day hike or an overnighter. Out on the trail, you'll hear something you don't hear much (quiet), encounter animal tracks, walk for miles without seeing anyone, and if you sleep over, see more stars than you ever imagined.

LONG •TRAIL

34. A Supernatural Sighting Spot

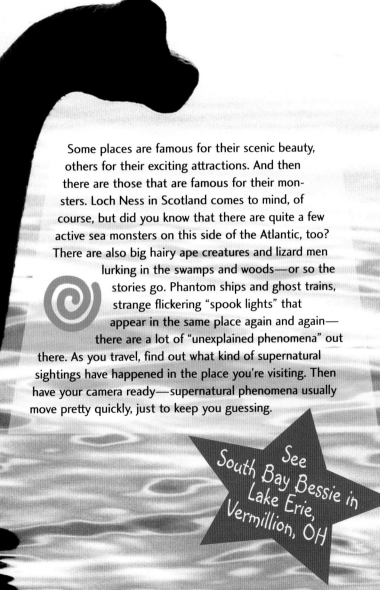

Some places are famous for their scenic beauty, others for their exciting attractions. And then there are those that are famous for their monsters. Loch Ness in Scotland comes to mind, of course, but did you know that there are quite a few active sea monsters on this side of the Atlantic, too? There are also big hairy ape creatures and lizard men lurking in the swamps and woods—or so the stories go. Phantom ships and ghost trains, strange flickering "spook lights" that appear in the same place again and again— there are a lot of "unexplained phenomena" out there. As you travel, find out what kind of supernatural sightings have happened in the place you're visiting. Then have your camera ready—supernatural phenomena usually move pretty quickly, just to keep you guessing.

See South Bay Bessie in Lake Erie, Vermillion, OH

35. An Old Folks' Home

You might think that you don't have a whole lot in common with old people: you're not exactly on the same energy level. What could you possibly do at an old folks' home that would be fun? How about talking? Pick your favorite subject. You like baseball? You might find someone who saw Jackie Robinson play ball, live, in person. Is music your thing? There's bound to be an old-timer around with a cool old collection of 78 records. Wonder what it was like to live through, or even fight in, World War II? Don't just read about it in a book—hear the story firsthand. People don't stop being interesting just because they're old. A long life means lots of great stories to tell: all you have to do is listen.

36. A Sculpture Park

It's like a museum without walls and without the try-to-keep-your-voice-down rule. No walls means nothing's too big to fit, so you'll see the most gigantic sculptures, and sometimes you can touch them or even climb on them (check the park's rules before you do, please). No walls also means the weather and the sculpture can interact: the wind blows movable parts, the sculpture casts cool shadows on the ground, snow rests on top of it, and rain makes its surfaces slick. The sculpture becomes part of the landscape, like a tree or a rock. And if the sculpture makes you want to do a cartwheel, go right ahead—try doing that in a museum!

Queen Califia's Magical Circle, by Niki de Saint Phalle, at Kit Carson Park, Escondido, California

37. A Farmers' Market

A farmers' market is about so much more than fresh vegetables (although those are pretty awesome). Depending on where you live, you might find: musical entertainment; handmade soaps and lotions; fresh honey with the honeycomb still in the jar; or homemade cider, jams, and jellies (and usually lots of free samples!). A farmers' market changes with the seasons, so you'll never see exactly the same place twice. There are bouquets of fresh-picked flowers in spring and summer, locally grown pumpkins for Halloween, and trees and wreaths as December approaches. A visit to a farmers' market is a great way to find out about what grows in your area and be close to your food source (see #6). And don't forget those free samples!

Check your local newspaper for information on where and when to find the best farmers' markets.

38. A Wetland ⊚

The Native Americans who lived near it called Florida's Everglades "the river of grass." Ecologists call it an inland marsh. River of grass is more poetic, but both terms describe a type of wetland—a place where earth and water constantly intermingle. The water nurtures plants, which in turn attract animals, making wetlands amazingly diverse habitats. There are lots of different types of wetlands—marshes, bogs, fens, swamps, vernal pools, playas, wet meadows, and prairie potholes. Some are in unexpected places (near New York City or Las Vegas), and each is teeming with all different kinds of life, from hermit crabs in the salt marshes to alligators in the swamps. Wild, mysterious, and yes, even poetic—wetlands are definitely a must-see.

39. A Pigpen

For generations, possibly centuries, parents have used the pigpen as the ultimate example of untidiness and slovenly behavior. Cries of "Clean up your room! It looks like a pigpen!" have rung out in homes large and small, in countries all over the world. But what exactly does a pigpen look like? Are kids all over the world the victims of an unjust comparison? Or is it the pigs that have been unfairly accused? See for yourself whether the comparison between your room and a pigpen has any merit. You may be surprised to find that pigs are quite a bit tidier than they're given credit for (and perhaps you are, too). They're also kind of sweet and cute, so they're worth a visit anyway.

40. An Ancient City

The cliff dwellings at Mesa Verde National Park date to around A.D. 1200.

Greek temples, Egyptian pyramids, and Aztec cities are oh-so-fascinating, but oh-so-far-away. Did you know there are lots of places where you can explore ancient civilizations right here in North America? Earthworks; effigy mounds shaped like bears, snakes, and other animals; cliff dwellings; and pueblo ruins all offer a look into North American life centuries before European settlers arrived. Standing in a place where people conducted ceremonies or just played stickball thousands of years ago, you can just feel the history. How were the people who lived here like you and how were they different? Thousands of years from now, will a kid stand in what was once your backyard and wonder the same thing?

41. A Battlefield

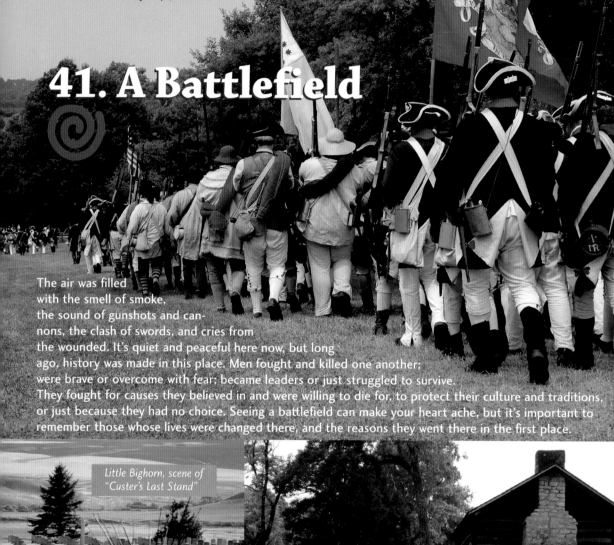

The air was filled
with the smell of smoke,
the sound of gunshots and can-
nons, the clash of swords, and cries from
the wounded. It's quiet and peaceful here now, but long
ago, history was made in this place. Men fought and killed one another;
were brave or overcome with fear; became leaders or just struggled to survive.
They fought for causes they believed in and were willing to die for, to protect their culture and traditions,
or just because they had no choice. Seeing a battlefield can make your heart ache, but it's important to
remember those whose lives were changed there, and the reasons they went there in the first place.

Little Bighorn, scene of
"Custer's Last Stand"

The battlefield at Chickamauga and
Chattanooga National Military
Park, Fort Oglethorpe, Georgia

42. A Boardwalk

COTTON CANDY

If you're taking your exploring seriously, you've already been to the uninhabited island mentioned in #10. For a completely different beach experience, you need to see a boardwalk. Boardwalks are kind of old-timey and that's the fun of them. They have hot dog stands, sno-cones, carnival rides, fortune-tellers, and silly souvenirs. But the best part is the people watching. Something about being on a boardwalk brings out the wackiness in people: you might see flame-eaters, roller-skating musicians, people juggling strange things like chainsaws. Where else can you get all this…and for free?

43. A REPAIR SHOP

Cars, appliances, cameras, bicycles, you name it—everything breaks. And somebody, somewhere, knows how to fix it. If you're the kind of kid who has to take everything apart to see how it works, you've really got to see a repair shop. When your parents take the car in for repairs, ask whether you can take a look as the mechanics put it up on a lift or get under the hood. When your bike needs fixing, ask if you can watch the bike mechanic do the work. Watch as your washing-machine repair person pulls tubes and wires out and puts everything back together again. Who knows, *you* may even figure out how to put something you took apart back together again.

44. A Folk Or Junk Art Creation

One person's trash is another person's treasure. Some really interesting people devote their whole lives to piecing together what others call junk to make indescribable artistic statements. They're not trained artists: they use bits of whatever—bottles, cans, broken glass, scrap metal—for art supplies. It's not the kind of stuff you usually see in a museum: a sky-piercing cathedral of bicycle parts, a painted concrete fantasy world, acres and acres of spinning whirligig contraptions. You won't believe it until you see it, and you may even be inspired to create some amazing art of your own.

The Forevertron (above) is just one of dozens of amazing scrap metal sculptures that can be found in the "Land of Evermor" near Baraboo, Wisconsin.

45. A Great Estate

They called it "the gilded age"—a time in the late nineteenth century when the richest of the rich liked to live large and show off their money. They built spectacular mansions featuring priceless works of art, private bowling alleys, indoor swimming pools, and grand ballrooms. They had hundreds of servants who came running at the ring of a bell, and dumbwaiters that spirited food in and out of their banquet halls. Although you probably wouldn't have scored an invitation to one of these homes back then, today—you're in! Imagine what it was like to live in all that splendor—even the servant's quarters weren't too shabby.

Hearst Castle in San Simeon, California, was the home of newspaper tycoon William Randolph Hearst. Now it's part of the California State Parks system.

Williamstown GENERAL STORE
COUNTRY STORE & DELI

46. GENERAL STORE

Back in the old days before shopping centers and strips malls, there were general stores. They were the only store in town, and you could get everything you needed there: food, fabric for making clothes, shoes, school supplies—you name it. But it wasn't so much the stuff that made general stores special—it was the atmosphere. You could always count on running into someone you knew there (hopefully someone you liked!) and you could always catch up on the latest news. The general store was really at the heart of the community. Although many have vanished, there are still some great general stores left that you can visit. They still have really cool merchandise that you won't find anywhere else, but best of all, they still have *atmosphere*.

47. A Forest Canopy

Looking up from the forest floor at the dappled sunlight filtering down through a canopy of leaves is a beautiful experience. But can you imagine what the view is like from the top, what it must be like to see as the birds see, soaring above the tree-tops? In a few rare and wonderful places, you can do just that. Climb to the top of a forest, and then walk on a swinging bridge through the trees or zip along the forest canopy on a harness and wire, like a bird in flight. In the few years they've been studying the forest canopy, scientists have discovered tons of new species. It's like a whole secret world up there, and being among the treetops is an experience you'll never forget.

Walk or zip through the forest canopy at Cypress Valley Canopy Tours in Spicewood, Texas.

48. A Gateway to the New World

They came from China, Poland, Ireland, the Ukraine, Sweden, or Italy. They left everything they knew behind, looking for a better life in "the New World." Every immigrant has a unique story, and you can learn about those stories in the places where they first arrived in North America. Get an idea what they experienced, see their pictures, and maybe even discover something about your own family. No matter where your ancestors came from, the immigrants' story is part of your story, because every group that came to North America affected the others as they forged new nations together.

"Picture brides" from Japan arrived at Angel Island in San Francisco Bay in the early part of the 20th century.

49. A Big Dune

THESE
700-FOOT-
HIGH DUNES AT
GREAT SAND DUNES
NATIONAL MONUMENT ARE
NORTH AMERICA'S HIGHEST.

A barrier island, a mountain of sand, a shifting desert: sand dunes take different shapes in different places. In coastal areas, they're fragile: each year the sea claims a little bit more of them. You can look, but you can't walk on them. Even a little human activity can harm them. In desert areas, they can stand up to anything. You can hike up, roll down, or even "sandboard" across them. And even though the wind constantly reshapes them, they remain more or less in the same place for years. Lovely to look at or fun to play on, sand dunes are definitely worth a visit.

50. A Haunted Place

Wet footprints near a dry indoor pool, ghostly crew members—
The haunted Queen Mary, docked in Long Beach, California

*Magnificent.
Mysterious. Haunted?
The Banff Springs
Hotel, Banff, Alberta*

There's no guarantee that you're going to see a ghost when you visit a place that's said to be haunted. But at least you've got a better chance than you do at a place that's not supposed to be haunted. Every town has its share of haunted places, so you probably won't have to go far to find one. But whatever you do, don't go alone, at night, under a full moon, or any of that silly scary movie stuff (and definitely don't trespass on private property—that makes the ghosts *and* the owners mad). Whether or not you believe in ghosts, it's interesting to visit a "haunted" place because at the very least you'll hear a good ghost story that you can repeat to your friends around the campfire one dark, spooky night.

*Myrtles Plantation in St. Francisville, Louisiana—
"the most haunted home in America"*

Close your eyes and breathe in—aaaaahh! What an amazing sweet-y, musky, savory smell—like a bouquet of flowers and a fresh-baked pizza all at once! Where are you? In a sensory garden. Sensory gardens are designed so that people who can't see can still enjoy a garden through their other senses. But anyone can go to one. They're especially good to visit after you've been stuck in a classroom all day breathing in chalk dust—instant sensory rejuvenation. Leave behind the world of drab white walls, hard desk seats, and fluorescent lights, and enter an oasis full of flowers in a rainbow of colors, some with fuzzy leaves to touch, or even herbs that you can break off and taste. And what about the sounds? Rustling grasses, chirping birds, wind chimes, or trickling fountains. You'll feel totally reenergized—isn't it amazing that plants can do that?

Check with your local botanical garden or horticultural society to locate a sensory garden near you. Or better yet, make one of your own. Check out this site for ideas: www.kidsgardening.com.

52. A Literary Location

Mark Twain's famous character Tom Sawyer once said "There ain't anything that is so interesting to look at as a place that a book has talked about." Bad grammar aside, Tom has a point. Seeing a literary location up close is really cool. Do you love the *Little House* books by Laura Ingalls Wilder? Visit the real little houses. (Laura moved a lot!) How about *From The Mixed-Up Files of Mrs. Basil E. Frankweiler?* Visit the museum where Claudia and her brother lived. Find out about the lives of famous writers, ones you know and others you might not know yet. And when you go home, sit down and write about it!

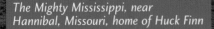

The Mighty Mississippi, near Hannibal, Missouri, home of Huck Finn

53. An Amazing Architectural Achievement

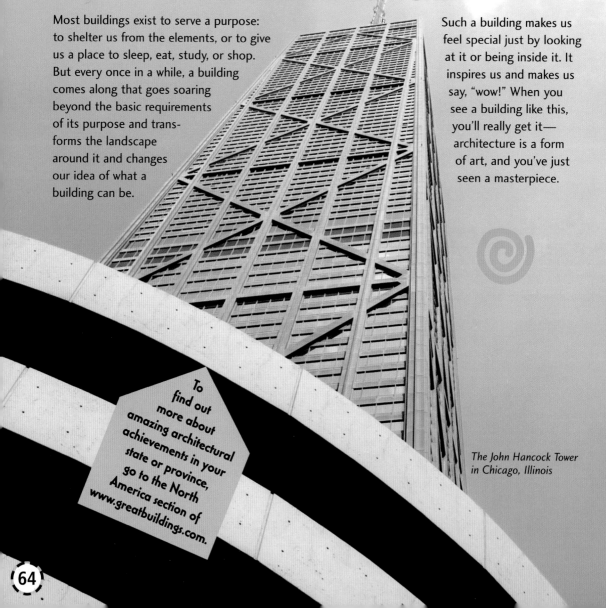

Most buildings exist to serve a purpose: to shelter us from the elements, or to give us a place to sleep, eat, study, or shop. But every once in a while, a building comes along that goes soaring beyond the basic requirements of its purpose and transforms the landscape around it and changes our idea of what a building can be.

Such a building makes us feel special just by looking at it or being inside it. It inspires us and makes us say, "wow!" When you see a building like this, you'll really get it—architecture is a form of art, and you've just seen a masterpiece.

The John Hancock Tower in Chicago, Illinois

To find out more about amazing architectural achievements in your state or province, go to the North America section of www.greatbuildings.com.

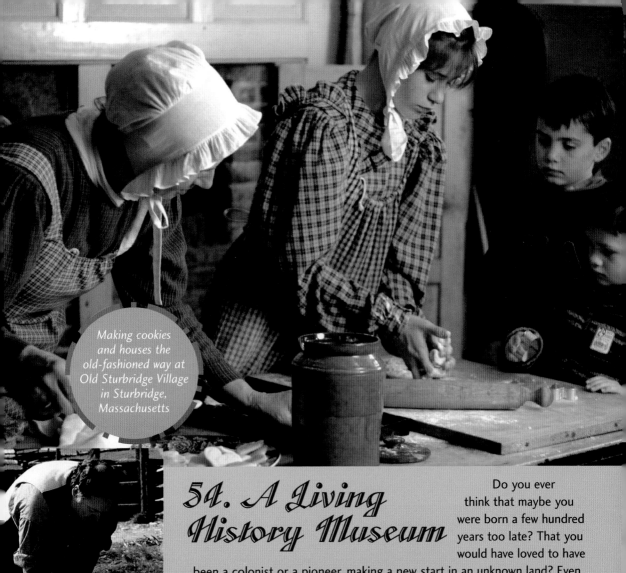

Making cookies and houses the old-fashioned way at Old Sturbridge Village in Sturbridge, Massachusetts

54. A Living History Museum

Do you ever think that maybe you were born a few hundred years too late? That you would have loved to have been a colonist or a pioneer, making a new start in an unknown land? Even if you're just a tiny bit curious, you gotta see a living history museum. It's a place where not just the buildings and objects, but also the way of life from another time, have been preserved for you to experience. You'll see how people did everyday things, what they ate, wore, and did for fun… and, yes, it was possible to have fun before video games.

For information on living history museums in almost every state and province, go to **www.alhfam.org/alhfam.links.html**

55. A Place of Worship
(other than your own)

The Sikh temple in Vancouver

A boy makes his bar mitzvah, a Jewish rite of passage.

Most kids would agree that what the world needs now is a little more peace and understanding. But what can a kid do, and how can you start? Well, you can start by getting to know people who are different from you so you can better understand their culture or beliefs. Visit a place of worship that's different from your own to find out what it's all about. Attend a service or ask your host to explain the symbols, rituals, and beliefs to you. One of the most surprising things you'll probably learn is that we all have a lot more in common that we think.

FAITH FACTS

• There are more than 200 Hindu temples in North America.
• The oldest synagogue in North America, Touro Synagogue in Newport, Rhode Island, was built in 1763. It also houses the oldest Torah in North America.
• The largest mosque in North America is in Dearborn, Michigan.
• The Buddhist Church in San Francisco is the oldest Buddhist temple in North America.
• The Cathedral of St. John the Divine in New York City, a "house of prayer for all nations" is the world's largest cathedral and has been under construction for over 100 years.

56. A GREENWAY

Inside the heart of every city kid lays a tree-hugging, fresh air breathing, nature lover just waiting to break free. But, where to go in the concrete jungle to get in touch with your inner outdoorsy kid? Get yourself to a greenway! What's a greenway? It's an urban trail, usually along a river or waterfront, designed to connect city-dwellers with nature. In-line skaters, bikers, runners, and walkers can all do their thing on a greenway without having to worry about traffic. And as an added bonus, greenways let nature do its thing, too: native plants and critters abound. You'll feel like you're a million miles away from the city even if you've only traveled a few blocks.

57. A Very Big Thing

Legendary lumberman Paul Bunyan and his blue ox Babe are larger-than-life reminders of the famous American tall tale about their adventures. This Bunyan and Babe are in Bemidji, Minnesota, but you can find others like them in the following locations:

California   Klamath and Porterville
Idaho   Coeur d'Alene
Maine   Bangor (Paul Bunyan's birthplace)
Michigan   St. Ignace
Minnesota   Akeley (the world's largest Paul Bunyan), Bemidji, and Brainerd
New York   Lake George and Old Forge
Oklahoma   Aline
Wisconsin   Minocqua and Eau Claire

BEMI
PAUL
BUNYAN
1937

In a big country, people think big: big houses, big cars, big meals, big…talking farm animals? All over this great big land, people have made it their goal to make the very biggest …something in the world. Because if a catsup bottle is good, doesn't it stand to reason that a giant catsup bottle is better? At the very least, it's going to get your attention. As you explore, keep your eyes open for very big things. They're very easy to spot: that's the point. How many can you find?

The World's Largest Catsup Bottle can be found in Collinsville, Illinois.

A very big, very pink dinosaur greets you at Stan's Dinosaur Land in Vernal, Utah, which also claims to be "The Dinosaur Capital of the World."

69

⊙ 58. A Fort

In the Middle Ages, they had castles. In colonial and frontier North America, they had forts. Forts kept settlers or army forces in, and the enemy of the moment (it often changed) out. Forts were built to withstand anything, and many of them have survived battles, bombardment, and natural disasters. Since you don't have to worry about cannon fire or arrows coming at you, you can walk along the battlements and check out the views (forts are usually built on the highest ground around). And if you get the idea that it would be really hilarious to dangle your little brother over the side, please try to control yourself.

Bent's Old Fort near La Juncta, Colorado was a busy trading post for settlers and Native Americans on the Santa Fe Trail.

The gentle long-necked Apatosaurus (seen in the replica below) wouldn't have stood a chance against T-Rex jaws like these.

59. A Dinosaur Site ◎

All of North America was once dinosaur country, and dinosaurs left their mark (well, their bones and footprints, really) all over the place before they disappeared forever. A visit to a dinosaur site or museum is as close as you can get to seeing what they were like in real life. You can look at reconstructed skeletons and life-size reproductions, and maybe even take part in a dig yourself. It's amazing how many different types of dinosaurs there were (and scientists are discovering an average of seven new kinds each year). If you are, or ever were, dino-crazy, you've just gotta check out a dino-site.

60. A First-Rate, Secondhand Store

Let's face it: your allowance probably doesn't go as far as it used to. So what's a cash-poor kid to do? Go to a secondhand store! You'll find unique (sometimes strange) stuff that no one else has, and you can add to a collection or even start a new one. Sure, you might have to dig around a lot of junk to find it, but don't give up—it's the possibility that you might come away with a real treasure that makes secondhand stores so much fun.

61. An Unusual Museum

Meet the Trashosaurus, made entirely of recycled materials, at the Children's Garbage Museum in Stratford, Connecticut.

There are certain things that come to mind when one thinks of a museum. Art? Definitely. Historical objects? Perhaps. garbage? Probably not. And yet, there is a garbage museum, and it happens to be just for kids. There's also a museum devoted to the pets of American presidents. If you're into intrigue, there's a Cold War museum, a spy museum, and a cryptological museum. If you're into small, burrowing animals (and who isn't?), there's a gopher museum. Aluminum Christmas trees, shells, angels—the list goes on and on. Even if you don't consider yourself the museum type, get yourself to an unusual museum for a very unusual experience.

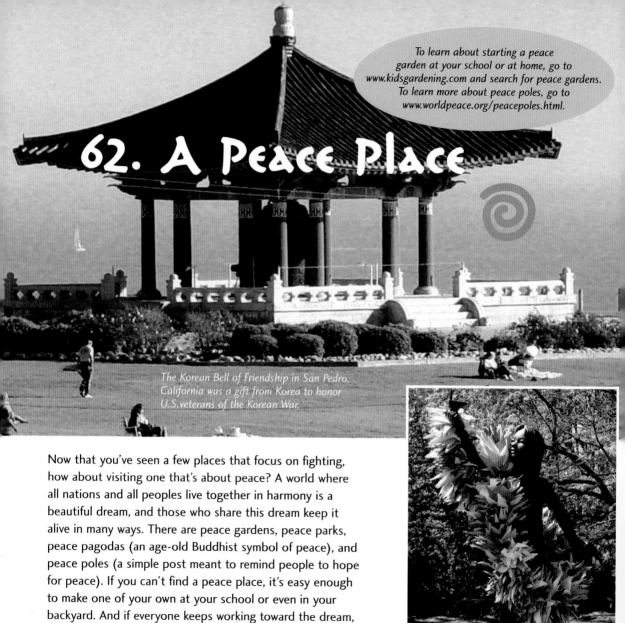

62. A Peace Place

To learn about starting a peace garden at your school or at home, go to www.kidsgardening.com and search for peace gardens. To learn more about peace poles, go to www.worldpeace.org/peacepoles.html.

The Korean Bell of Friendship in San Pedro, California was a gift from Korea to honor U.S. veterans of the Korean War.

Now that you've seen a few places that focus on fighting, how about visiting one that's about peace? A world where all nations and all peoples live together in harmony is a beautiful dream, and those who share this dream keep it alive in many ways. There are peace gardens, peace parks, peace pagodas (an age-old Buddhist symbol of peace), and peace poles (a simple post meant to remind people to hope for peace). If you can't find a peace place, it's easy enough to make one of your own at your school or even in your backyard. And if everyone keeps working toward the dream, every place can be a peace place.

Sadako Sasaki, a Japanese girl exposed to radiation during the bombing of Hiroshima, became an international ambassador for peace when she started a campaign to fold 1,000 paper cranes as a symbol of her wish for peace. Visit her statue at the Sadako Peace Park in Seattle, Washington.

"I will write peace on your wings and you will fly all over the world."
—Sadako Sasaki

74

63. The Teachers' Lounge

Every school has one—that top-secret, off-limits, inner sanctum known as the teachers' lounge. What exactly is it that they do in there, you wonder. Perhaps they sit around cackling like witches, coming up with cruel and unusual homework assignments? What's in there anyway? A locked cabinet full of voodoo dolls with students' faces on them? A complete set of the three-volume classic, *How to Be Boring?* You'll never know unless you take a peek. You can do it legally (help a teacher carry some stuff back there one day) or just sneak a glance through the door between classes. In the end, you may find that it's just a regular old room where teachers grade papers and drink coffee—or is that just what they *want* you to think?

64. A Stargazing Spot

Through all of human history, they've always been there, twinkling in the sky, constant and unwavering, no matter what happens down here on Earth. They're beautiful and mysterious, challenging us to try to reach them, always beyond our grasp. Stars inspire us, give us hope somehow, and make us feel like we're not alone in the vast universe. See these captivating sky-dwellers up close (well, as close as you can, really) through a high-power telescope at a planetarium or an observatory. Check out the giant telescopes that can see light years away and dishes that can hear into deep space. No matter how much you find out about stars, there will always be more to learn, and there will always be new mysteries to discover.

See the world's largest collection of optical telescopes at Kitt Peak National Observatory in the Sonoran desert south of Tucson, Arizona.

65.
A Newsroom

What exactly is news? Who decides what we hear about and what we don't? How does the news circulate? What's the difference between local and national news? Visit your local newspaper, radio, or TV station to get "the real scoop." You may be able to meet with a reporter or an editor, see a newspaper being printed, or watch anchor people reading the news live. Like a good reporter, you should ask a lot of questions so that you really understand what you're seeing. Some media offer public tours; others may let you visit if you make an appointment. Either way, make sure you follow up on these leads and get the whole story.

66. Backstage of a Theater

From your seat in the audience, you see actors transformed into animals, witches, or royalty. You watch as they fly through the air or suddenly appear from out of the floor. You see cityscapes or enchanted forests glide on and off the stage, as if by magic. So, what's the secret behind these amazing spectacles? Go backstage and find out. There are "shops" full of props and dazzling costumes and wigs, dressing rooms illuminated by lighted mirrors, set-building shops where ships or palaces are created from paint and plywood. There are hidden elevators and trapdoors that spirit the performers from place to place, and pulleys that let them fly. All this awaits you behind the curtains, so check it out.

67. A Mint

Have you ever heard the expression "Money doesn't grow on trees?" Well, it's true—money is made in a mint, and you can actually watch it happening. Find out how designs are developed, models are created, and coins are engraved and "struck." It's really cool to watch millions of newly minted coins just pouring out of a machine or giant blank pieces of paper turn into dollar bills. Even though they have lots of cash around, they're not giving it away—if you want it, you're still going to have to earn it.

See *billions* of dollars being printed at the Bureau of Engraving and Printing in Washington, D.C.

Pain au chocolat
(chocolate croissant)

Palmier (giant crispy
pastry, also known as an
"elephant ear")

Éclair (cream-filled pastry
with chocolate sauce on top)

Crème Brûlée (crusty
custard dessert)

Mont Blanc (creamy
meringue desert with
chestnut flavoring)

Croissant (flaky pastry,
often served with filling such
as raspberry, almond, or
chocolate)

Mille feuille (Napoleon)
(flaky layered pastry, often
with cream filling between
the layers)

Chocolat moelleux
(dense chocolate cake)

Tarte tatin (apple tart)

Tartalette citron (lemon tart)

Religeuse (Puff pastries
covered with icing and stacked
on one another)

Profiteroles (little cream puffs,
often covered with a chocolate
sauce)

68. A Patisserie

Works of art aren't always made to be looked at; some are meant to be eaten. A *patisserie* (an authentic French pastry shop) is like a gallery of edible art. The artist in the kitchen is a *patissière* (a pastry chef) who uses age-old techniques and only the freshest ingredients to make her masterpieces. While you're sleeping, patissières are working through the night so that the pastries are fresh and ready the next morning. All that hard work is obvious when you look inside the patisserie's glass case at flaky pastries with "millions" of layers, raspberry or lemon-filled tarts, or little chocolate mice with eyes and whiskers made of icing. The pastries are so beautiful that it's almost a shame to eat them. But go ahead—they're *très bon!*

Look in your local phone book to find a patisserie near you.

69. A RADICAL ROCK FORMATION

Nature is a better sculptor than humans could ever hope to be—it just takes its time creating its works of art. Nature uses wind and water as its tools, wearing away a little bit of rock or stone every year until it creates a fantastic sculpture. It may take tens of thousands (or even millions) of years to complete, but what's the rush? Nature has all the time in the world. Nature's radical rock formations sometimes resemble something we recognize (such as the Dinosaur or Elephant Rock) and sometimes look like something from outer space (such as the hoodoos and badlands of the west). Either way, you just gotta see them.

Pioneers dubbed this valley in Utah Goblin Valley because of the **hoodoos** (strange, weathered rocks like these ones) and other spooky rock formations that dominate the landscape.

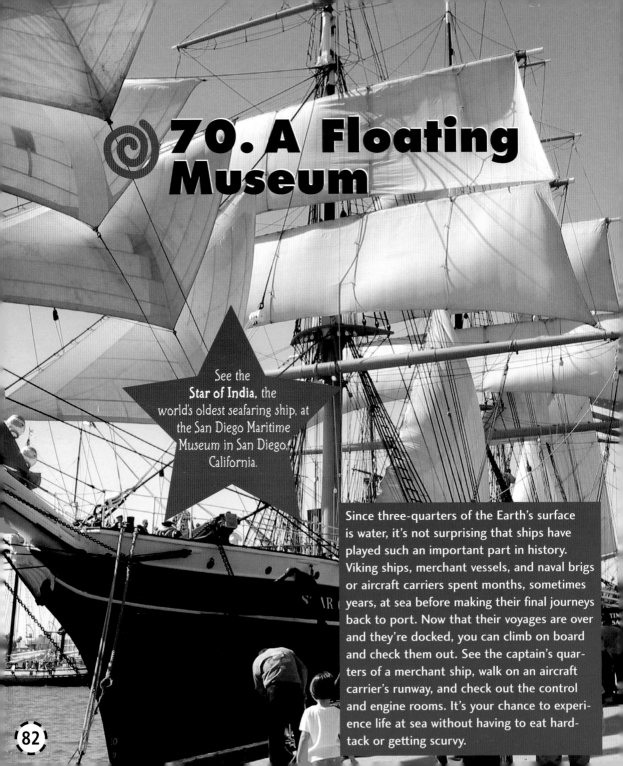

70. A Floating Museum

See the **Star of India**, the world's oldest seafaring ship, at the San Diego Maritime Museum in San Diego, California.

Since three-quarters of the Earth's surface is water, it's not surprising that ships have played such an important part in history. Viking ships, merchant vessels, and naval brigs or aircraft carriers spent months, sometimes years, at sea before making their final journeys back to port. Now that their voyages are over and they're docked, you can climb on board and check them out. See the captain's quarters of a merchant ship, walk on an aircraft carrier's runway, and check out the control and engine rooms. It's your chance to experience life at sea without having to eat hardtack or getting scurvy.

71. An Archeological Site

To find an archeological site near you, check out the listings at *Dig* magazine's Web site: www.digonsite.com/guide.

We think we know a lot about the past. And then one day, a farmer is plowing a field and hits an object. It's something that doesn't seem to belong there—a part of a skull, a tool, maybe a shard of pottery. He has it examined, and everything we thought we knew changes. The farmer's field, it turns out, is on the site of an old village, one no one knew about. And as layers of dirt are removed, the village reappears, and we discover a forgotten part of the past. New archeological sites are being found all the time—in the middle of cities, in the countryside, maybe even in your town. Not only can you see one, but at many sites, you can actually help dig. You could be the one to find an important piece of history. And even if you don't, you'll have fun digging in the dirt.

72. A HALL OF FAME

Everybody is good at *something*. But at a hall of fame, you can learn about those who are the very *best* at what they chose to do. It's inspiring to learn the stories behind your favorite athletes, musicians, inventors, or even dancers. (And if you visit during induction weekend, you may even get to meet them.) It can be even more interesting to learn about the stars you've never heard of (they have great stories, too). There are halls of fame for just about every endeavor you can think of, and some dedicated to some pretty strange stuff (cockroaches, robots, and hamburgers, to name a few). Who knows? Maybe you'll be in one some day.

The First Class

Learn about baseball legends at the Baseball Hall of Fame in Cooperstown, New York.

Walk through the amazing giant Muskie at The Freshwater Fishing Hall of Fame in Hayward, Wisconsin.

73. An Artist's Inspiration

Monet had Giverny; Van Gogh had his fields of sunflowers. Artists draw inspiration from the world around them—from nature or even from simple things they encounter in their day-to-day lives. Visit a place that's often been the subject of artists' work, and capture it artistically in your own unique way. Or visit an artist's home and studio to see the places that inspired his or her creations. It's cool to compare how the place looks in real life with the way the artist captured it on canvas, paper, or film. Then again, you could just find a place that inspires you—someday, when you're a famous artist, it will be known as the place where you did your "early work."

74. An Unusual Animal Farm

Bison, emus, ostriches, llamas, and alpacas: Old McDonald never had *these* on his farm. However, some farmers do, and it's fun to see them. There's really nothing like the sight of hundreds of enormous woolly bison grazing on a hill together or the sound of a peacock mating call (it's way louder than you would think!). And who can resist the sight of a friendly, fluffy llama? Unlike at a zoo, you get to observe the animals up close at an animal farm. Rules permitting, you may even get to interact with them and find out the answer to that eternal question: Do llamas really spit?

75. A Courthouse

The courthouse is usually the most impressive building in town—big Greek columns on the front, maybe a rotunda on top. It has to look very serious because important things happen there—people get married, file legal documents, or go to trial. With so many momentous events happening under its roof, a courthouse is a very dramatic place (that's probably why so many TV shows are based there). Sign up for a courthouse tour and see lawyers and judges in action. Observe jury selection, an arraignment (when people find out what charges have been brought against them), or even a trial. Ask questions if you can't figure out what's going on. You'll get a close-up view of the justice system in action, and you'll be really glad you're on the right side of the law.

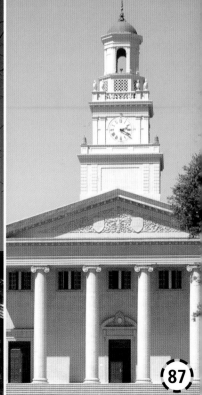

76. A WORKING PORT

A giant cruise ship glides slowly past a rusty old fishing boat; a freighter with a name written in an unknown script sits at dock as workers unload huge containers of who-knows-what bound for who-knows-where; a fancy yacht raises its sails and heads out into open water—a port bustles with activity day and night, bringing together people (and boats!) from around the world. There are fishing ports where you can watch fishermen unload their catch of the day and cargo ports where you can watch stevedores unload cars from Germany or containers of goods from China. No matter which one you see, the intersection of land and sea is a fascinating place to be.

Cargo ships from Asia, cruise ships bound for Alaska, pleasure boats, and commuter ferries all converge in the Port of Seattle.

77. A Replica

There's nothing like the real thing, they say. But whoever *they* are, they haven't seen a replica—a thing that exists simply to be *like* the real thing. The Eiffel Tower, the *David*, even planet Earth—have all been re-created for your viewing convenience. So, in case you never quite make it to Paris, Florence, or outer space to see these famous sites, you can still see something that is *almost* just like the real thing.

Can't get to Paris, France? See a replica of the Eiffel Tower in Paris, Texas.

A replica of the Wright Brothers' 1902 glider, the first successful airplane, is on view at the Wright Brothers National Memorial in Kitty Hawk, North Carolina. This one was flown at Wright Patterson Air Force Base in Ohio.

See a Viking ship replica at L'Anse Aux Meadows National Historic Site in St-Lunaire-Griquet, Newfoundland.

© 78. AN INVENTIVE PLACE

When asked about his hundreds of inventions, Thomas Edison famously replied that for every one that was successful, there were thousands that had failed. The key, he said, was that each mistake helped him get closer to success. Thanks to Edison's persistence, we now have the electric light bulb, recorded music, movie cameras, and many other things that make life easier. Inventors are some of the most interesting people in history and the places where they developed their new ideas are cool to visit—fascinating old laboratories filled with gadgets, devices, and plans for changing the world. Visit an inventive place—a lab, workshop, or even the U.S. Patent and Trademark Museum—to learn more about inventors and their amazing achievements.

Edison Labs, in West Orange, New Jersey—the place where motion picture cameras and nickel-iron-alkaline storage batteries were invented.

79. An Endangered Place

You've heard of endangered species, right? They are animals so few in number that their entire species might cease to exist. Well, animals aren't the only things that can disappear—places can, too. Historic buildings, landmarks, and even whole neighborhoods or geographic areas face destruction from neglect, development, and environmental factors. And when they do, a little bit of our history and culture disappears with them. Nothing lasts forever, but some places are so special that they deserve to be saved. Visit an endangered place, and imagine what it would be like if your kids never got to see it. Then see what you can do to help.

Grain elevators, the skyscrapers of the prairies, are forgotten and falling to pieces.

Prairie churches were once the heart of new immigrant communities but now many are abandoned.

To learn more about endangered places, check out the National Trust for Historic Preservation (U.S.) at www.nationaltrust.org or the Canadian Conservation Institute at www.cci-icc.gc.ca. Or look at the World Monument Fund's list of 100 Most Endangered Places at www.wmf.org.

80. A Special Place to Sleep

Well, by now you've done quite a bit of exploring, and that probably means you've stayed in a few hotels. It's exciting at first, but after a while it can start to seem like you've seen this place before: the boring room with the two double beds, the "continental breakfast" in the morning, consisting of a Danish pastry in a plastic bag and little mini-boxes of cereal. It may be time to get some more excitement from your lodgings. How about sleeping in a lighthouse? A tree house? A castle? What about a hotel made of ice? There are lots of lodgings where just staying there is an experience in itself. You may just decide to stay up all night to enjoy it and not go to sleep at all.

Stay in the Ice Hotel near Québec City, Québec, open from January until around April (when it starts to melt). Artists create a new one each year, with special features including ice furniture, ice chandeliers, and fantastic ice sculptures.

81. A Place Where They Make Cool Stuff

If you've ever tried to make anything yourself, you know how hard it can be to get it just right. Whether it's a batch of cookies or a model airplane, if one little thing goes wrong, you might not get the results you want. That's why it's so interesting to visit a place where products are made—whether it's potato chips or guitars—to see how they get things done. You can watch as wax is turned into crayons, or see big vats of gloppy sugar made into candy. Find out what makes airplanes, cars, and snowboards move, and what keeps them from falling apart. Your tour guide will explain how everything works, and you may just learn a few tips that you can use in your own creative endeavors.

82. An Ethnic Restaurant

Dinner at a sushi restaurant isn't just a meal—it's a cultural experience!

Spanish paella—spicy rice is nice

Souvlaki, "the hamburger of Greece"

Are you the kind of kid that thinks French fries are a foreign food and eating pizza counts as having an Italian meal? Take your tastebuds on a trip to a faraway land of fascinating flavors. Try *sushi* (Japanese), *dim sum* (Chinese), or *baba ghanoush* (Middle Eastern). Don't be daunted by unfamiliar names—think of yourself as a brave explorer and your meal as a culinary expedition. If you're already into adventurous cuisine, try going a little further afield. There's Ethiopian food—you use spongy bread called *injera* to scoop up your food instead of using a fork or spoon. Or *bulgogi*—Korean barbeque. It's cooked right at your table, which has a kind of grill in the center. At an ethnic restaurant, you'll learn about different cultures, not just food. You may not love everything you try, but you just might develop a taste for something other than pizza.

the Original

BIRD CAGE THEATRE

of Tombstone

83. A Legendary Location

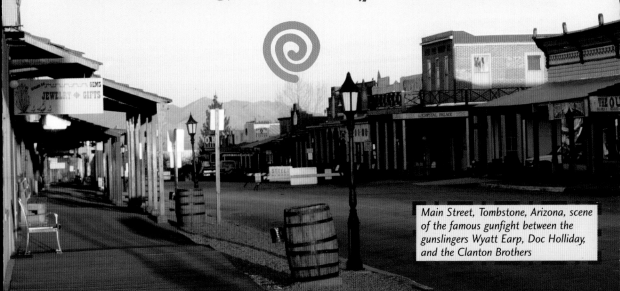

Main Street, Tombstone, Arizona, scene of the famous gunfight between the gunslingers Wyatt Earp, Doc Holliday, and the Clanton Brothers

The Alamo. The OK Corral. Chances are that even if you don't know what happened there, you've heard of these legendary places. Through the years, the stories about their history has been embellished so much that no one can say for sure what's fact and what's fiction. So make a visit and try to sort it out for yourself. See a re-enactment of the Boston Tea Party at the Old South Meeting House in Boston, or of the shoot-out at the OK Corral in Tombstone. Visit Sleepy Hollow, the place where the headless horseman was said to have made his legendary ride. Being in a such a legendary place makes you feel like you're part of history.

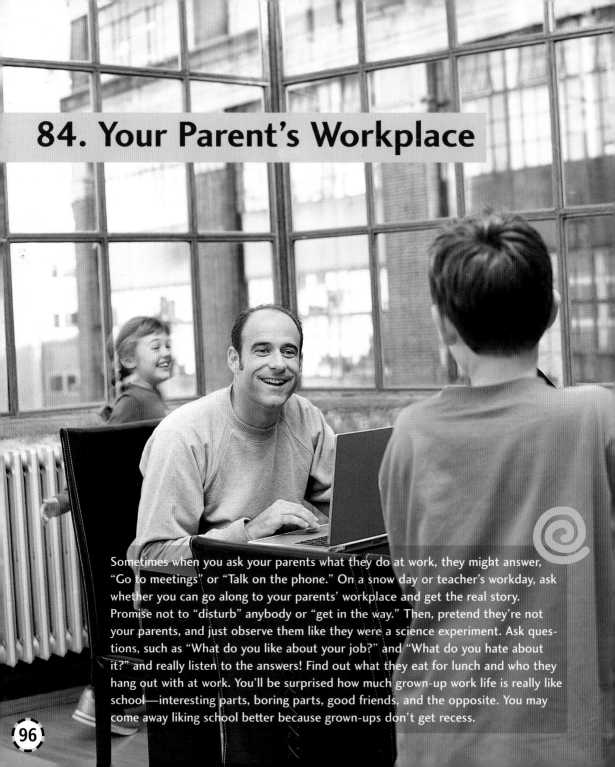

84. Your Parent's Workplace

Sometimes when you ask your parents what they do at work, they might answer, "Go to meetings" or "Talk on the phone." On a snow day or teacher's workday, ask whether you can go along to your parents' workplace and get the real story. Promise not to "disturb" anybody or "get in the way." Then, pretend they're not your parents, and just observe them like they were a science experiment. Ask questions, such as "What do you like about your job?" and "What do you hate about it?" and really listen to the answers! Find out what they eat for lunch and who they hang out with at work. You'll be surprised how much grown-up work life is really like school—interesting parts, boring parts, good friends, and the opposite. You may come away liking school better because grown-ups don't get recess.

al St, Lispenard St
v of the Americas
24 hour booth

The New York City Subway—Ride the trains or take a special tour of abandoned stations through the New York Transit Museum in Brooklyn.

85. A Subway

London has "the Tube." Paris has "the Metro." Boston simply calls its underground train system "the T." In every great city (and even some not so great ones) there's a whole world underneath your feet—a subway system. Most people just see it as a way to get from point A to point B, but you can learn a lot about a city from its subway, and the cool thing is that every city's subway is different. Watch who gets on and off the train at different stations—you'll see shoppers at some, business people or students at others. Check out the art and read the maps posted in the stations or eavesdrop on your fellow passengers' conversation (just be discreet). You'll have such a good time, you may just miss your stop.

86. A Canyon or Gorge

When you hear the word "canyon," the first thing you think of is "grand." In fact, the Grand Canyon is *so* grand that all the other canyons in North America have kind of an inferiority complex because of it. Quite a few canyons are so anxious to be favorably compared to the Grand Canyon that they call themselves "the grand canyon of" a certain area, just so that everyone knows they are impressive as well. The truth is that there are many, many canyons and gorges that, were it not for the Grand Canyon, would be considered quite grand in their own right. You really must see the Grand Canyon one day, but in the meantime, why not pay a visit to one of the less famous but truly spectacular canyons? The canyon will be grateful that you remembered it, and you'll see an amazing sight.

"The Grand Canyon of Hawaii," Waimea Canyon

An old apothecary shop full of herbal cures at Colonial Williamsburg, Williamsburg, Virginia

They want to suck your blood—from ancient times until the 19th century, leeches were used to break fevers and relieve inflammation.

87. A Medical Museum

You may not always like the taste of the medicine you're given, but consider the alternative: if you'd been born 100 years ago, you might have been given leeches. Not to eat, of course, just to suck your blood to remove the impurities from it. Through the years, medical researchers have made a lot of discoveries that make it easier for us to stay healthy, but they had to try a lot of wacky ideas before getting it just right. Visit a medical museum to learn about what used to happen when someone got sick. You'll see jars full of old herbal medicines, old medical instruments, and maybe even some bottles with dead or live leeches. In some of the creepier exhibits, you'll see human skulls and skeletons, or actual human organs preserved in fluid. You'll never complain about having to go to your doctor's office again.

88. AN AIRPLANE HANGAR OR COLLECTION

The Great Gallery of the Museum of Flight in Seattle, Washington is a six-story-tall steel and glass structure that houses 39 historic aircraft.

You've probably seen one in the movies, but have you ever seen one in person? An airplane hangar is likely to be the biggest building you've ever been in. In fact, certain hangars (such as the ones created for blimps) are so large they're said to create their own weather systems. Even if you don't see one that big, you'll get to see airplanes in a very different way than you do when you're riding in one. Your local private airport may host an "open hangar day," or you may be able to set up a tour. If you can't, try to check out an airplane museum or collection that's not in a hangar. Any building that's big enough to park an airplane inside has to be impressive.

89. A Prison or Jail

For some reason, law-abiding citizens love to visit jails. In fact, Alcatraz, the famous prison on an island in San Francisco Bay, is one of the most visited tourist attractions in all of California (and there are a lot of amazing places to visit in California)! So what is it about jails that's so intriguing? Make a visit to one and find out. You'll learn the true stories behind some of history's most notorious criminals, discover escape plots, see weapons made out of soap, and take a chilling glance into the cells where convicts waited out their sentences. You'll also learn a lot about the justice system and how it has changed through the years. And you'll leave feeling very glad you're not required to stay.

90. A Hero's Home

Brave. Determined. Inspiring. Unforgettable. Those are all words that describe the greatest leaders, the people whom we know as heroes. They come from different backgrounds—some rich, some poor, some well educated, others self-made. But somehow they became people that we've all heard of and admire. When you visit the home of a hero, you learn something about his or her story and contributions to history. But more than that, you leave with the impression that one person really can change the world, and that's reason enough to try.

Lincoln Homestead State Park in Springfield, Kentucky

91. A School That's Different from Yours

Going to school is probably the last thing you want to do with your time off. But if you go to a school that's not yours, it can be really interesting. For you, there are tests, no grades, and definitely no homework—what could be bad? You can just check out what's going on and see which things are alike, different, better, and worse than your own school. If you go to a public school, visit a private one. If you go to a private school, visit a public one.

If you're home-schooled, visit either kind. Spend a few hours at a school for the blind or deaf, or one where the teaching takes place in another language. Ask a friend who goes to the school to show you around (otherwise they probably won't let you in). In the end, either you'll be glad you go to your school or you'll ask your parents to transfer you to the new one.

92. A Famous Road

Route 66 is so famous, it's got a song about it—"Get Your Kicks on Route 66."

Roads are sometimes called arteries because they lead to the heart of a city. And like real arteries, some roads seem to have a pulse—they have their own special energy and make a city feel alive. What would Paris be without the Champs-Elysées? Or Barcelona without the Ramblas? Some day, you'll get to those famous streets, but in the meantime, check out some legendary roads closer to home. Some are best experienced on foot, others by car. But you're guaranteed to see something interesting. There's a famous road in every town—have you been to one in yours?

Shop till you drop on Rodeo Drive in Los Angeles.

93. A People-Watching Place

If you were a psychologist or sociologist, you'd call it "conducting behavioral research." But since you're just an ordinary kid, you can call it people watching: sitting back and observing what the people around you are doing, what they're wearing, what they're saying. You can really do it any-where, but every town has a place that is especially "good for people watching." It might be a park, a certain street, or even the mall. Pick a good spot, get yourself something to eat or drink, and just watch. Don't stare, of course—that will make you too obvious (and would be rude). The key to people watching is to blend in with the background so that no one is watching you. Stay as long as you're interested, then move along—it's that easy.

94. An Amazing Science Site

At Fermilab National Accelerator Laboratory in Batavia, Illinois, physicists tackle the big questions: What is the universe made of? How does it work? Where did it come from? Ask a scientist for answers on a special tour of the lab.

If science were sports, the scientists who work in these labs would be the major league players. We would follow their every move as they researched subatomic particles, and go nuts when they knocked one out of the park with a really great advancement in physics. In reality, these science superstars achieve great feats without much cheering and not a single endorsement from an athletic shoe company. But that doesn't make what they do, such as develop new sources of energy, map the human genome, and basically unlock the secrets of the universe, any less amazing. Because what scientists do is so sensitive (and in some cases top secret), you can't just walk in and ask to look around. But you can prearrange a tour (often with a school group) or attend an open house—it's like getting a ticket to the world series of science.

95. An Eccentric Eatery

When you've been out on the road traveling for a while, you can get a bit bored and hungry. You could stop at the same old drive-through, but why? There are lots of restaurants that are destinations in and of themselves. You can eat in a flying saucer, in a cave on Mars, or in a rain forest. You can watch cliff divers or jousting tournaments as you nibble. You can pull your dinner off a miniature train that brings it to your table or catch it as your server throws it at you. Eccentric eateries have so much atmosphere that eating is almost an afterthought (but they have pretty good food, too).

At Casa Bonita in Denver, you can watch cliff divers and flame jugglers and listen to strolling mariachis while you eat or explore the restaurant's lost mines and caverns.

If you're ever in southeastern Missouri, stop by Lambert's Café, "Home of the Throwed Rolls." If you order rolls, they will indeed be thrown at you.

You can't miss it—billboards for hundreds of miles on I-95 announce the location of the South of the Border restaurant in Dillon, South Carolina, where you can eat Mexican food and ride to the top of the 'sombrero tower' in a glass elevator.

96. The Middle of Nowhere

It's not a place that can be mapped, but you'll know it when you see it. You'll be riding along in a car, on a bus, or in a train. Looking out the window, you'll see—well, not much. Someone who you're traveling with will say, "Where are we? The middle of nowhere?" The trick is, at this point, to stop and find out where you really are. Because even the middle of nowhere is really somewhere, and it may be more interesting than you thought. Try to find out the name of the place, what it's known for, whether anyone lives there, and if so, what they do. Even if it turns out that the middle of nowhere is not that interesting after all, at least you can say you've been there.

It's the most talked about thing in the world: the weather. It affects everyone, every day—what we wear, what we do, even where we live. Considering how important the weather is, we don't always know that much about it. But there are meteorologists working hard to predict it, and in some places, you can see them in action. Check out all the amazing storm-tracking equipment they use and learn about pressure systems or climate change. Just for fun, you might also want to visit the most famous unofficial meteorologists in the world, too—a couple of weather-predicting groundhogs (make sure you stop by on February 2nd or you might not catch them above ground).

97. A Weather Spot

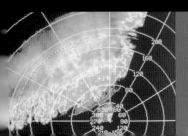

Learn about tornados, thunderstorms, thunder and lightning at National Severe Storms Laboratory in Norman, Oklahoma (see page 134 for more info).

98. A Recording Studio

Rocker. Rapper. Diva. Do you dream of becoming a star? If you spend a good amount of time in front of the mirror singing into a hairbrush, you really have to see a recording studio. Find out what a mixing board looks like, what record producers and sound engineers really do, and how they achieve all those cool sound effects. Some studios specialize in voice-overs and commercial advertising, while others focus on music of all kinds, from classical to pop or country. You may be able to watch a recording session, and if you're lucky, you might even get to lay down a track of your own.

Check your local phone directory to find out about recording studios in your town, then call up and tell them you're interested in seeing their facilities.

To find a greenhouse near you, check your local phone directory or do an Internet search.

99. A Greenhouse

Outside the weather is cloudy and cold, the trees are bare, and there's not a speck of green to be seen. But step inside the doors of a greenhouse, and a rush of warm tropical air and a riot of colors greet you. You've been transported, not just through space, but also through time; it's another season in here. Greenhouses can expertly re-create the climate of a place that may be very far away, indeed: the Amazonian rain forest, an arid desert, or a plant bog. You can see rare orchids, spiny cacti, and even carnivorous plants as bright tropical frogs leap over your path and macaws squawk in the trees above you. When your visit is over, you probably won't want to go back outside into your own environment. But you can always return for a little blast of summer when you've got the winter blues.

100. A Street Market

Painter for the People

From the exotic *souks* of Marrakech to London's famed Portobello Road, street markets are the liveliest spots in any town. Even on an ordinary day, it feels like something exciting is happening there. The streets are lined with stalls selling anything from inexpensive jewelry to books, toys, or interesting little objects you've never seen before. There's usually music in the air, and the smells, tastes, and colors of everything for sale make it oh so much more than just a shopping experience. *Haggling* (asking for a better price) is a tradition at street markets, so if you find something you really want, don't let a high price tag get you down. Offer a lower price and let the negotiations begin! Even if you don't purchase anything, you'll leave with a great memory.

101.A Really Cool Place That You Discover All On Your Own

Call this one an 'extra credit' place, if you like. Find a place, a place unlike the others in the book, a place you stumble upon in your travels or one you find through careful research. It could be a famous place or a spot in your backyard, in the middle of a city or out in the wilderness, near home or very far away. The important thing is that it's an interesting and special place to you. Take your time discovering your place (since this is extra credit, you can even wait till after you're 12 if you need to). Write it down on your list or keep it a secret. Then congratulate yourself for your discovery— you're now officially an explorer.

The Lists

There wasn't room to include all the great places in North America, but the lists on the following pages are a start at helping you locate places to see close to home and in other regions. These aren't necessarily the biggest, most famous, or best of all places. (Only you can decide what you think is the best.) They're a mix—some places everyone's heard of (The Grand Canyon, for example) and others that are more like "hidden gems" for you to discover. You can find an art museum in your state or a radical rock formation near your grandma's house, a literary location in your neighborhood, or a wetland near the place where you're going on vacation. Use the abbreviations list on the right and the map inside the back cover to help you locate places. Search the websites listed for more information about each place. Do some research on your own to discover even more places to explore. Take this book with you when you travel so you can build in some side trips, or design a whole trip around the places!

Abbreviations

United States

Alabama: AL
Alaska: AK
American Samoa: AS
Arizona: AZ
Arkansas: AR

California: CA
Colorado: CO
Connecticut: CT

Delaware: DE
District of Columbia: DC

Florida: FL

Georgia: GA

Hawaii: HI

Idaho: ID
Illinois: IL
Indiana: IN
Iowa: IA

Kansas: KS
Kentucky: KY
Louisiana: LA

Maine: ME
Maryland: MD
Massachusetts: MA
Michigan: MI
Minnesota: MN
Mississippi: MS
Missouri: MO
Montana: MT

Nebraska: NE
Nevada: NV
New Hampshire: NH
New Jersey: NJ
New Mexico: NM
New York: NY
North Carolina: NC
North Dakota: ND

Ohio: OH
Oklahoma: OK
Oregon: OR

Pennsylvania: PA

Rhode Island: RI
South Carolina: SC
South Dakota: SD

Tennessee: TN
Texas: TX

Utah: UT

Vermont: VT
Virgin Islands: VI
Virginia: VA

Washington: WA
West Virginia: WV
Wisconsin: WI
Wyoming: WY

Canadian Provinces

Alberta: AB

British Columbia: BC

Manitoba: MB

New Brunswick: NB
Newfoundland and Labrador: NL
Northwest Territories: NT
Nova Scotia: NS
Nunavut: NU

Ontario: ON

Prince Edward Island: PE

Quebec: QC

Saskatchewan: SK

Yukon: YT

1. LIGHTHOUSES

Portland Head Light
Cape Elizabeth, ME
www.portlandheadlight.com

Cape Hatteras Light Station
Cape Hatteras, NC
www.nps.gov/caha/lh.htm

Seul Choix Point Lighthouse
(said to be haunted!)
Gulliver, MI
www.greatlakelighthouse.com

Pigeon Point Light Station
Pescadero, CA
www.parks.ca.gov, search Pigeon Point Light

7. SPACE PLACES

Smithsonian National Air and Space Museum
Washington, DC
www.nasm.si.edu

U.S. Space and Rocket Center
Huntsville, AL
www.spacecamp.com/museum

Kennedy Space Center
Cape Canaveral, FL
Watch rocket launching
www.nasa.gov/centers/kennedy

Johnson Space Center
Houston, TX
Mission Control, astronaut training center
www.nasa.gov/centers/johnson

9. ANIMAL RESCUE CENTERS

The Elephant Sanctuary
Hohenwald, TN
www.elephants.com

Karen Beasley Sea Turtle Rescue
Center
Topsail Island, NC
www.seaturtlehospital.org

Big Cat Rescue
Tampa, FL
www.bigcatrescue.org/kids_tours.htm

The Montana Large Animal Sanctuary and Rescue
Hot Springs, MT
Llamas, bison, sheep, pigs, and others
www.mtanimalsanctuary.com

The Marine Mammal Center
Sausalito, CA
Sea lions, seals, sea otters, whales, and dolphins
www.tmmc.org

10. FARAWAY ISLANDS

St. Lawrence Islands National Park
Mallorytown, ON
www.pc.gc.ca/pn-np/on/lawren

Cumberland Island, GA
www.nps.gov/cuis

Saint Vincent National Wildlife Refuge
Island four miles from Apalachicola, FL
www.fws.gov/saintvincent

Apostle Islands
Lake Superior, WI
www.nps.gov/apis

Channel Islands, CA
www.nps.gov/chis

Gulf Islands National Park Reserve
Sidney, BC
www.pc.gc.ca/pn-np/bc/gulf

12. OLD-GROWTH FORESTS

Southern Five Pond Wilderness Adirondack State Park
Paul Smiths, NY
www.northnet.org/adirondackvic

Joyce Kilmer Memorial Forest
Robbinsville, NC
www.main.nc.us/graham/hiking/
joycekil.html

Isle Royale National Park
Houghton, MI
www.nps.gov/isro

Great Basin National Park
Baker, NV
Ancient bristlecone pines
www.nps.gov/grba

Redwood National and State Parks
Crescent City, CA
Some trees may be 2,000
years old!
www.nps.gov/redw

13. GHOST TOWNS
Cockburn Island, ON (ghost island)
www.ghosttowns.com/canada/ontario/cockbur-
nisland.html

Portsmouth Island,
NC
Ghost island
www.portsmouthis-
land.com/village.html

Nicodemus, KS
www.nps.gov/nico

Rhyolite, NV
www.rhyolitesite.com

Bodie, CA
www.bodie.com

Silver City, ID
www.ghosttowns.com/states/id/silvercity.html

Bannack, MT
www.bannack.org

14. WATERFALLS
Niagara Falls
Niagara Falls, NY and ON
www.niagrafallsstatepark.com
www.city.niagarafalls.on.ca

Land of the Waterfalls
Brevard, NC
www.waterfalls-guide.com/nc_waterfalls-guide.htm

Tahquamenon Falls State Park
Paradise, MI
www.michigandnr.com/parksandtrails

Yosemite Falls
Yosemite National Park, CA
The highest falls in North America
www.nps.gov/yose

Athabasca Falls, Jasper National Park
Jasper, AB
www.pc.gc.ca/pn-np/ab/jasper/visit/visit29_e.asp

15. OLYMPIC TRAINING CENTERS
U.S. Olympic Training Center
Lake Placid, NY
www.usoc.org/12181_19094.htm

Lakeshore Foundation
Birmingham, AL
Training site for Olympics, Special Olympics, and
Paralympics
www.lakeshore.org

Pettit National Ice Center
Milwaukee, WI
www.thepettit.com

U.S. Olympic Training Center
Colorado Springs, CO
www.usoc.org/12181_19096.htm

ARCO Training Center
Chula Vista, CA
www.chulavista.com/sub/arco.htm

Canada Olympic Park
Calgary, AB
www.canadaolympicpark.ca/activities/tours.asp

17. KOOKY CAPITALS
Snack Capital of the World, Hanover, PA
Home of numerous pretzel and potato chip facto-
ries (which give tours and free samples)
http://www.yorkpa.org, go to For Kids

Killer Bee Capital of the World
Hidalgo, TX
The place where killer bees
crossed the border into the
United States; home to the
world's largest killer bee (a
statue)
www.roadsideamerica.com/attract/TXHIDbee.html

Troll Capital of the World
Mount Horeb, Wisconsin
Named for the troll traditions of Norwegian settlers
http://www.trollway.com/mounthoreb.asp

Polar Bear Capital of the World
Churchill, MB
Home to the largest polar bear calving ground
www.polarworld.com

Bigfoot Capital of the World
Willow Creek, CA
Birthplace of Bigfoot hunting; bigfoot collection in
local museum
www.unmuseum.org/bigfoot.htm

Dinosaur Capital of the World
Drumheller, AB
Home of Dinosaur Valley and "the world's largest
dinosaur"
www.dinosaurvalley.com

18. ART MUSEUMS
Montréal Museum of Fine Arts
Montréal, QC
www.mmfa.qc.ca/en

Metropolitan Museum of Art
New York, NY
www.metmuseum.org

High Museum of Art
Atlanta, GA
www.high.org

Art Institute of Chicago
Chicago, IL
www.artic.edu/aic

J. Paul Getty Museum
Los Angeles, CA
www.getty.edu

Legion of Honor
San Francisco, CA
www.legionofhonor.org

19. ROCK ART SITES
Petroglyphs Provincial Park
Peterborough, ON
www.ontarioparks.com/english/petr.html

Crystal River Archeological State
Park
Crystal River, FL
www.floridastateparks.org

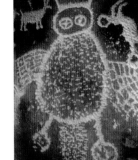

Canyonlands National Park
Moab, UT
www.nps.gov/cany

Canyon de Chelly National
Monument
Chinle, AZ
www.nps.gov/cach

Writing-on-Stone Provincial Park
Near Milk River, AB
www.cd.gov.ab.ca, search Writing On Stone

20. WIND FARMS
Searsburg Wind Power Facility,
Searsburg, VT

Storm Lake Wind Power Generation Facility
Storm Lake, IA

Wind Power Learning Center
Lake Benton, MN

The American Wind Power Trail
Northwest Texas and southern Oklahoma
Nearly 20 wind farms in one region
www.windpowertrail.com

Wind Farms of the Tehachapi Pass
Kern County, CA

San Gorgonio Pass, CA

Stateline Wind Energy Center
Oregon-Washington border, near Pendleton, OR and
Touchet, WA

21. AQUARIUMS
Parc Aquarium du Québec, QC
www.spsnq.qc.ca

New England Aquarium
Boston, MA
www.neaq.org

Georgia Aquarium
Atlanta, GA
www.georgiaaquarium.org

Great Lakes Aquarium
Duluth, MN
www.glaquarium.org

Monterey Bay Aquarium
Monterey, CA
www.mbayaq.org

22. "LITTLE" COUNTRIES OR CITIES
Toronto, ON
  Little India
  Chinatown
  Corso Italia (Italian)
  Greektown (largest in North America)
  Portugal Village
  Little Poland
  Koreatown

New York, NY
  Chinatown
  Little Italy (Mulberry
  Street, Manhattan)
  Little India (Jackson Heights, Queens)
  Middle Eastern neighborhood (Atlantic Avenue,
  Brooklyn)
  Greek neighborhood (Astoria, Queens)
  Little Odessa, Russian (Coney Island, Brooklyn)

Thunder Bay, ON
  Little Finland

Miami, FL
  Little Havana (Cuban)

Chicago, IL
  Little Italy
  Chinatown
  Pilsen/Little Village (formerly Czech, German,
  Polish, Croatian, and Lithuanian, now one of the
  largest Mexican communities in the U.S.)
  Greektown

Winnipeg, Manitoba
  Chinatown
  Mosaic Market
  French Quarter
  Selkirk (Ukranian)

Los Angeles, CA
  Chinatown
  Koreatown
  Little Persia (Iranian)
  Little Tokyo
  Olvera Street (historic Mexican neighborhood)

San Francisco, CA
  Chinatown (the largest Chinatown outside of Asia)
  Japantown
  North Beach (Italian neighborhood)

23. CRAZY DREAM HOUSES
Gillette Castle
East Haddam, CT
http://dep.state.ct.us/stateparks/parks/gillettecas-
tle.htm

Historic Loveland Castle
Loveland, OH
www.lovelandcastle.com

Coral Castle
Homestead, FL
www.coralcastle.com

House on the Rock
Spring Green, WI
House jutting out of a cliff ramp, an enormous fire-
place, and secret rooms
www.thehouseontherock.com

Scotty's Castle Death Valley National Park
Death Valley, CA
www.usparkinfo.com/deathvalley.html

Winchester Mystery House
San Jose, CA
Eccentric mansion with 160 rooms
www.winchestermysteryhouse.com

25. FAMOUS FIELDS
Lamade Stadium
South Williamsport, PA
Home of the Little League World Series
www.littleleague.org, search Lamade Stadium

Fenway Park
Boston, MA
Home of the Boston Red Sox and America's oldest
and "most beloved" ballpark
http://boston.redsox.mlb.com, go to Fenway Park

"Field of Dreams"
Dyersville, IA
Where the baseball movie was filmed
www.fieldofdreamsmoviesite.com

Wrigley Field
Chicago, IL
Home of the Chicago Cubs
http://chicago.cubs.mlb.com, go to Wrigley Field

Dodger Stadium (Chavez Ravine)
Los Angeles, CA
Home of the Los Angeles Dodgers
www.ballparks.com/baseball/national/dodger.htm

26. BIG CAVES
Scenic Caves
Collingwood, ON
www.sceniccaves.com

Mammoth Cave National Park
Mammoth Cave, KY
The longest cave in the
world!
www.nps.gov/maca

Wyandotte Caves
Marengo, IN
www.wyandottecaves.com

Jewel Cave
Custer, SD
www.nps.gov/jeca

Timpanogos Cave National Monument
American Fork, UT
www.nps/gov/tica

Carlsbad Caverns
Carlsbad, NM
www.nps.gov/cave

27. GEYSERS AND NATURAL HOT SPRINGS
Warm Mineral Springs, FL
www.warmmineralsprings.com

Hot Springs National Park
Hot Springs, AR
www.hot.springs.national-park.com

Evans Plunge
Hot Springs, SD
www.evansplunge.com

Hot Springs all over New Mexico!
www.discovernewmexico.com/hotsprings

Strawberry Park Hot Springs
Steamboat Springs, CO
www.strawberryhotsprings.com

Hot Springs State Park
Thermopolis, WY
http://wyoparks.state.wy.us/hsslide.htm

Sharkey Hot Springs
Tendoy, ID
www.idahohotsprings.com/destinations/sharkey

Temple Gardens Mineral Spa Resort
Moose Jaw, SK
www.templegardens.sk.ca

Ainsworth Hot Springs Resort
Kootenays, BC
www.bchotsprings.com

29. INSECTARIUMS
Montréal Insectarium
Montréal, QC
www2.ville.montreal.qc.ca/insectarium/insect.htm

Philadelphia Insectarium
Philadelphia, PA
More than 100,000 insects, many alive
www.gophila.com/culturefiles/Museums/insectarium

Audubon Insectarium, Audubon Nature Institute
New Orleans, LA
www.audubonzoo.com/insect

Monsanto Insectarium,
Saint Louis Zoo
Saint Louis, MO
www.stlzoo.org

Insect Zoo, Kansas State University
Manhattan, KS
www.k-state.edu/butterfly

Insect Zoo, San Francisco Zoo
San Francisco, CA
www.sfzoo.org, search Insect

Victoria Bug Zoo
Victoria, BC
www.bugzoo.bc.ca

30. MARVELS OF ENGINEERING
CN Tower
Toronto, ON
The world's tallest freestanding
structure
www.cntower.ca

Empire State Building
New York, NY
The tallest building in the world for 40 years; now
the tallest in New York City
www.esbnyc.com

St. Louis Gateway Arch
St. Louis, MO
630-foot-high inverted
catenary curve
www.greatbuildings.com/
buildings/Gateway_Arch.html

Hoover Dam
Thirty miles south of Las
Vegas, NV
www.usbr.gov/lc/
hooverdam/service

Golden Gate Bridge
San Francisco, CA
The world's tallest suspension bridge
www.pbs.org/wgbh/amex/goldengate

31. CEMETERIES
Old Burying Ground
Halifax, NS
Famous for "gravestone art"

Arlington National Cemetery
Washington, DC
Graves of several presidents and the Tomb of the
Unknown Soldier

Boot Hill Cemetery
Dodge City, KS
Many famous gunslingers who died "with their
boots on"

Saint Louis Cemetery No. 1
New Orleans, LA
Marie Laveau, the voodoo queen, plus many eigh-
teenth-century crypts

Hollywood Forever Cemetery
Los Angeles, CA
Prominent film industry figures

32. WILDLIFE REFUGES
Maine Coastal Islands National Wildlife Refuge
Milbridge, ME
Artic terns, Arctic puffins, and bald eagles
www.fws.gov/northeast/mainecoastal/history.html

Chincoteague National Wildlife Refuge
Chincoteague, VA
More than 300 species of birds, wild ponies
www.fws.gov/refuges/profiles, search Chincoteague

Florida Panther National Wildlife Refuge
Naples, FL
Place where Florida panthers den, hunt, and travel
www.fws.gov/floridapanther

National Bison Range
Moiese, MT
www.fws.gov/bisonrange/nbr

National Elk Refuge
Jackson, WY
More than 7,500 elk during
the winter months
www.fws.gov/nationalelkrefuge

33. LONG TRAILS
Bruce Trail
From Beamsville to Wiarton, ON
www.brucetrail.org

Appalachian Trail
From Springer Mountain, GA to Katahdin, ME

Ice Age Trail
A thousand-mile trail through Wisconsin
www.iceagetrail.org

North Country Trail
From northern NY, around the Great Lakes, to the
Canadian border in northern MI
www.northcountrytrail.org

Continental Divide Trail
From NM near the Mexican border, through the
Rocky Mountains, to AB at the Canadian border
www.cdtrail.org

Pacific Crest Trail
From the Mexican border in Southern CA, through
CA, OR, and WA, to the BC border in Washington
www.pcta.org

34. SUPERNATURAL SIGHTING SPOTS
The "Burning Ship" (phantom ship)
Northumberland Strait, between NS and PE

Champ, the Lake Champlain Monster
Lake Champlain (NY, VT, QC)

Brown Mountain Lights
Near Morganton, NC

Skunk Apes
Everglades and other swampy areas of Florida

South Bay Bessie (sea monster)
Lake Erie, Vermillion, OH

The *Edmund Fitzgerald* (sunken ship)
Seen in Lake Superior (sank in 1975)

Area 51 (UFO sighting spot)
Near Rachel, NV
"Top secret" government facility where alien craft is
said to have been stored

Caddy ("Cadborosaurus" sea serpent)
Cadboro Bay, Victoria, BC

Sasquatch (Bigfoot)
Willow Creek, CA and Creston, BC

36. SCULPTURE PARKS
Dr. Seuss National Memorial Sculpture Garden
Springfield, MA
Favorite Dr. Seuss characters in bronze
www.catinthehat.org/memorial.htm

Storm King Art Center
Mountainville, NY
The "mecca" of sculpture parks
www.stormking.org

Franconia Sculpture Park
Shafer, MN
www.franconia.org

Queen Califia's Magic Circle Garden
(Kit Carson Park)
Escondido, CA
www.queencalifia.org

di Rosa Preserve
Napa, CA
www.dirosapreserve.org

38. WETLANDS
Point Pelee Marsh
Near Leamington, ON
www.pc.gc.ca/pn-np/on/pelee

Everglades National Park
Homestead, FL
www.nps.gov/ever

Cache River State Park Natural Area, Vienna, IL
http://dnr.state.il.us, search Cache River State Park

Oak Hammock Marsh
Near Stonewall, MB
www.ducks.ca/ohmic

Big Thicket National
Preserve
Near Beaumont, TX
www.nps.gov/bith

Madrona Marsh
Preserve
Torrance, CA
www.friendsofmadronamarsh.com

40. ANCIENT CITIES
Moundville Archeological Park
Near Tuscaloosa, AL
Nearly 800 years ago, it was the largest city in
North America
http://moundville.ua.edu

Grand Village of the Natchez Indians
Natchez, MS
Main ceremonial center of the Natchez people from
around 700 to 1730
www.mdah.state.ms.us/hprop/gvni.html

Cahokia Mounds
Collinsville, IL
Largest Mississippian site, from 600 to 1500 AD
www.cahokiamounds.com

Mesa Verde National Park
Mesa Verde, CO
Indian cliff dwellings, almost a thousand years old
www.nps.gov/meve

Gila Cliff Dwellings National
Monument
Silver City, NM
One-time village nestled in
a cliff
www.nps.gov/gicl

41. BATTLEFIELDS
Concord's North Bridge, Minuteman National
Historical Park
Concord, MA(Revolutionary War)
www.nps.gov/mima

Antietam National Battlefield
Sharpsburg, MD (Civil War)
www.nps.gov/anti

Chickamauga and Chattanooga Battlefield
Fort Oglethorpe, GA (Civil War)
www.nps.gov/chch

Wilson's Creek National Battlefield
Republic, MO (Civil War)
www.nps.gov/wicr

Little Bighorn Battlefield National
Monument
Crow Agency, MT
www.nps.gov/libi

Kitwanga Fort
Queen Charlotte, BC (frontier
wars)
www.pc.gc.ca/lhn-nhs/bc/kitwanga/natcul

42. BOARDWALKS
The Beaches
Toronto, ON
www.wineva-oak.com

Coney Island, NY
www.coneyisland.com

Atlantic City, NJ
www.atlanticcitynj.com

Ocean City, Maryland
www.ocean-city.com/boardwalk
www.ocboards.com

Santa Cruz, CA
www.beachboardwalk.com

Santa Monica, CA
www.santamonicapier.org

44. FOLK OR JUNK ART CREATIONS
Pasaquan
Buena Vista, GA
www.pasaquan.com

The Land of Evermor
South of Baraboo, WI
Features The Forevertron, a scrap-metal contraption
(the largest in the world) plus a sculpture park
www.drevermor.com

Swetsville Zoo
Fort Collins, CO
Nearly 200 creatures made from car parts, scrap
metal, and farm machinery
www.roadsideamerica.com/attract/COFTCswetsville.
html

Cadillac Ranch
Amarillo, TX
www.antfarm.org

Watts Towers
Los Angeles, CA
Towering sculptures made from
junk; took 30 years to make
www.parks.ca.gov, search Watts Towers

45. GREAT ESTATES

Newport, RI, is home to many gilded age "summer
cottages," including:
– The Breakers, home of Cornelius Vanderbilt
– Marble House, home of William Vanderbilt
– Chateau-sur-Mer, home of China trade merchant
  William Shepard Wetmore
– The Elms, home of Edward Julius Berwind, coal
  mogul
– Kingscote, home of Southern planter George
  Noble Jones
– Rosecliff, home of Nevada silver heiress Theresa
  Fair Oelrichs
www.newportmansions.org

Biltmore Estate
Asheville, NC
Home of George Vanderbilt; the largest private
home in the United States
www.biltmore.com

Hearst Castle
San Simeon, CA
www.hearstcastle.com

Craigdarroch Castle
Victoria, BC
www.craigdarrochcastle.com

46. GENERAL STORES

Putney General Store
Putney, VT

St. James General Store
St. James, NY

32 Mott Street General Store (oldest store in
Chinatown)
New York, NY

Mast General Store
Valle Crucis, NC

Schwab Dry Goods Store
Memphis, TN

The General Store Museum
Cedarburg, WI

Kah Wah Chung Company Store
historic Chinesegeneral store
John Day, OR

Historic Kilby Store and Farm
Harrison Mills, BC

47. FOREST CANOPIES

Tree Canopy Walkway, EcoTarium
Worcester, MA
www.ecotarium.org

Haliburton Forest and Wild Life
Reserve
Haliburton, ON
www.haliburtonforest.com/
tour.htm

Myakka River State Park
Sarasota, FL
www.myakkariver.org

Cypress Valley Canopy Tours
Spicewood, TX
www.cypressvalleycanopy
tours.com/canopy-tours.php

Capilano Suspension Bridge Treetops Adventure
North Vancouver, BC
www.capbridge.com/ta/ta_banner.html

48. GATEWAYS TO THE NEW WORLD
Pier 21
Halifax, NS
The "gateway to Canada" for much of the twentieth century
www.pier21.ca

Ellis Island
New York, NY
More than 22 million people entered the United States through Ellis Island in the late nineteenth and early twentieth centuries
www.ellisisland.org

Museum of Westward Expansion
St. Louis, MO
Chronicles immigrants' journeys westward
www.nps.gov/jeff

Angel Island
San Francisco Bay, CA
Immigration station from 1910 to 1940
www.AngelIsland.org

49. BIG DUNES
Cape Cod National Seashore
Cape Cod, MA
www.nps.gov/caco

Cape Hatteras National Seashore
Outer Banks, NC
www.nps.gov/caha

Sleeping Bear Dunes National Lakeshore
Empire, MI
www.nps.gov/slbe

Great Sand Dunes National Park
Mosca, CO
www.nps.gov/grsa

White Sands National Monument
Holloman Air Force Base, NM
www.nps.gov/whsa

Guadalupe-Nipomo Dunes
Guadalupe, CA
www.dunescenter.org

Oregon Dunes National Recreation Area
Corvallis, OR
www.fs.fed.us/r6/siuslaw/recreation/tripplanning/oregondunes

Great Sand Hills
Sceptre, SK
www.cpaws-sask.org/prairie/great_sand_hills.html

50. HAUNTED PLACES
John Stone's Inn
Ashland, MA

Easton/Monroe Cemeteries, CT

Old Stone House Museum
Washington, DC

Shirley Plantation
Charles City, VA

The Gray Man of Pawley's Island, SC

Myrtles Plantation
St. Francisville, LA

Old Presque Isle Lighthouse
Presque Isle, MI

Hollenberg Station
Hanover, KS
The only remaining Pony Express station still in its original location

Old Deseret Village
Salt Lake City, UT

Pollard Hotel
Red Lodge, MT

Queen Mary Hotel
Long Beach, CA

Fairmont Banff Springs Hotel
Banff, BC

52. LITERARY LOCATIONS OR POETIC PLACES

Green Gables
Cavendish, PE
The home that inspired the setting for *Anne of Green Gables* by L.M. Montgomery
www.gov.pe.ca/greengables

Orchard House
Concord, MA
Home of Louisa May Alcott and inspiration for the home in *Little Women*
www.louisamayalcott.org

Chincoteague Island, VA
Home of *Misty of Chincoteague* by Marguerite Henry
www.imh.org/imh/bw/chinco.html

Mark Twain Museum
Hannibal, MO
Mark Twain's boyhood home and the home of Tom Sawyer in *The Adventures of Huckleberry Finn*
www.marktwainmuseum.org

Laura Ingalls Wilder Museum
Walnut Grove, MN
www.walnutgrove.org

Jack London's Ranch
Glen Ellen, CA
Home of the author of *Call of the Wild, White Fang, Sea Wolf,* and others
www.jacklondons.net/museum.html

53. AMAZING ARCHITECTURAL ACHIEVEMENTS

CN Tower
Toronto, ON
The world's tallest building (Architect: John Andrews)
www.cntower.ca

Solomon Guggenheim Museum
New York, NY
It's round! (Architect: Frank Lloyd Wright)
www.guggenheim.org

Milwaukee Art Museum
Milwaukee, WI
(Architect: Santiago Calatrava)
www.mam.org

Olympic Park
Montréal, QC
(Architect: Roger Taillibert)
An impressive inclined tower
www.rio.gouv.qc.ca/pub/parc/historique_po_a.jsp

Experience Music Project
Seattle, WA
Gehry's trademark free-form structure and shiny silver exterior walls (Architect: Frank Gehry)
www.emplive.org

54. LIVING HISTORY MUSEUMS

Sherbrooke Village, NS
Nineteenth-century village
http://museum.gov.ns.ca/sv/index.php

Old Sturbridge Village
Sturbridge, MA
Nineteenth-century town
www.osv.org

Colonial Williamsburg
Williamsburg, VA
Colonial city
www.history.org

Hale Farm and Village
Bath, OH
1848 township
www.canalwayohio.com/maps/halefarm.htm

Old World Wisconsin
Eagle, WI
Re-created Wisconsin immigrant village
www.wisconsinhistory.org/oww

Grant-Kohrs Ranch National Historic Site
Deer Lodge, MT
Ranching history site
www.nps.gov/grko

El Rancho de Las Golondrinas
Santa Fe, NM
Early New Mexico ranch
www.golondrinas.org

Motherwell Homestead
Abernethy, SK
Early twentieth-century farm
www.pc.gc.ca/lhn-nhs/sk/motherwell/index_e.asp

57. BIG THINGS
Giant mastodon
Stewiake, NS

Lucy the Elephant
Margate, NJ

The Big Chicken
Marietta, GA

World's largest baseball bat
Louisville Slugger Museum
Louisville, KY

Albert the (45-ton) Bull
Audubon, IA

World's largest catsup bottle
Collinsville, IL

Chatty Belle, world's
largest talking cow,
Neillsville, WI

Tommy the Giant
Turtle
Boissevain, MB

The Big Easel
Altona, MB

Giant fake dinosaurs
Cabazon, CA

The Freemont Troll
Seattle, WA

Mac, the World's Largest Moose
Moose Jaw, SK

World's largest dinosaur
Drumheller, AB

World's largest hockey stick and puck
Duncan, BC

58. FORTS
Old Fort Niagara
Youngstown, NY
(French and Indian wars and the Revolutionary War)
www.oldfortniagara.org

Fort Raleigh
Manteo, NC
Early English settlement
www.nps.gov/fora/about.htm

Castillo de San Marcos
Saint Augustine, FL
Early Spanish fortress
www.nps.gov/casa

Fort de Chartres
Near Prairie du Rocher, IL
Early French fort
www.swi-news.com/FortdeChartres.htm

Fort Scott National Historic Site
Fort Scott, KS
Cavalry post of the 1840s
www.nps.gov/fosc

Bent's Old Fort National Historic Site
La Juncta, CO
Trading fort
www.nps.gov/beol

Fort Langley National Historic Site
Fort Langley, BC
Trading post
www.pc.gc.ca/lhn-nhs/bc/langley/index_e.asp

59. DINOSAUR SITES
National Museum of Natural History
Smithsonian Institution
Washington, DC
www.mnh.si.edu

The Field Museum of Natural History
Chicago, IL
The largest T-rex
www.fieldmuseum.org

Rocky Mountain Dinosaur
Resource Center
Woodland Park, CO
www.rmdrc.com

Wyoming Dinosaur
Center and Dig Sites
Thermopolis, WY
www.wyodino.org

Dinosaurland
Vernal, UT
www.dinoland.com

Royal Tyrrell Museum
Drumheller, AB
www.tyrrellmuseum.com

61. UNUSUAL MUSEUMS
Children's Garbage Museum
Stratford, CT
Home of the trash-a-saurus, a dinosaur made of
trash
www.crra.org/pages/contact_garbage_museum.htm

International Spy Museum
Washington, D.C.
www.spymuseum.org

Presidential Pet Museum
Lothian, MD
www.presidentialpetmuseum.com

Bailey-Matthews Shell Museum
Sanibel Island, FL
More than 2 million shells in the "Great Hall of
Shells"
www.shellmuseum.org

City Museum
St. Louis, MO
Recycled art and art environments
www.citymuseum.org

The Science Fiction Museum and Hall of Fame
Seattle, WA
www.sfhomeworld.org

Gopher Hole Museum
Torrington, AB
www.bigthings.ca/alberta/torring.html

62. PEACE PLACES
Peace Garden at the Montréal Botanical Gardens
Montréal, QC
www2.ville.montreal.qc.ca/jardin, go to Gardens and
Greenhouses

United Nations
New York, NY
www.un.org/tours

International Peace Garden
Dunseith, ND and Boissevain, MB
www.boissevain.ca/attract/garden

Waterton-Glacier International
Peace Park
Waterton, AB and West Glacier, MT
www.nps.gov/glac

Sadako Peace Park
Seattle, WA
www.sadako.org/seattlepeacepark.htm

64. STARGAZING SPOTS
Planétarium de Montréal
Montréal, QC
www.planetarium.montreal.qc.ca

American Museum of Natural History
Rose Center for Earth and Space
New York, NY
www.amnh.org/rose

Morehead Planetarium, University of North Carolina
Chapel Hill, NC
www.moreheadplanetarium.org

Adler Planetarium and Astronomy Museum
Chicago, IL
www.adlerplanetarium.org

Kitt Peak National Observatory
Tohono O'odham Reservation, AZ
www.noao.edu/outreach/kptour

Very Large Array, National Radio Astronomy
Observatory
San Agustin, NM
 http://www.vla.nrao.edu

William Knox Holt Planetarium, University of
California at Berkeley
Berkeley, CA
www.lawrencehallofscience.org/planetarium

66. THEATERS WITH BACKSTAGE TOURS
Stratford Festival of Canada
Stratford, ON
www.stratford-festival.on.ca

Metropolitan Opera Guild
New York, NY
www.metoperafamily.org/education/calendar/back-
stage.aspx

The Fox Theater
Atlanta, GA
www.foxtheatre.org/tours.htm

Steppenwolf Theatre Company
Chicago, IL
www.steppenwolf.org

Kodak Theatre
Hollywood, CA
Home of the Oscars
www.kodaktheatre.com

67. MINTS
Royal Canadian Mint
Ottawa, ON
Makes commemorative coins, gold bullion coins,
medals, and medallions for circulation and commemorative purposes
www.mint.ca/royalcanadianmintpublic

Bureau of Engraving and Printing
Washington, D.C.
See billions of dollars and treasury notes being
printed!
www.moneyfactory.com

Denver Mint Facility
Denver, CO
Makes circulated and uncirculated coins and stores
gold and silver
www.usmint.gov

69. RADICAL ROCK FORMATIONS
Digby's Famous Balancing Rock
Digby, NS

Flowerpot Rocks
Hopewell Cape, NB
Carved by tides from the Bay of
Fundy

Old Man of the Mountain,
Franconia Notch State Park
Franconia, NH
Looks like a side of an old man's face

Natural Bridge
Natural Bridge, VA

Grandfather Mountain
Linville, NC

Stone Mountain
Stone Mountain, GA

Garden of the Gods
Shawnee National Forest, IL
Mushroom Rock, The Big H, and others

Miner's Castle, Pictured Rocks National Lakeshore
Munising, MI

Mount Rushmore
Keystone, SD

Lighthouse Rock and others
Palo Duro Canyon State Park
Near Amarillo, TX

City of Rocks State Park
Faywood, NM

Pikes Peak and Garden of the
Gods
Colorado Springs, CO

Devils Tower National Monument
Devils Tower, WY

City of Rocks National Reserve
Almo, ID

Goblin Valley State Park
Green River, UT

Bryce Canyon National Park
Bryce, UT

Monument Valley Navajo Tribal Park
Monument Valley, UT

Canadian Badlands
Drumheller, AB

70. FLOATING MUSEUMS
Mystic Seaport
Mystic, CT
Whaling ships
www.mysticseaport.org

Patriot's Point Navel and
Maritime Museum
Charleston, SC
U.S.S. Yorktown aircraft
carrier and several other
ships
www.patriotspoint.org

German U-505, Museum
of Science and Industry
Chicago, IL
German World War II sub-
marine
www.msichicago.org/exhibit/U505

U.S.S. Lexington, Lady Lex Museum on the Bay
Corpus Christi, TX
World War II aircraft carrier
www.hnsa.org/ships/lexington.htm

Star of India, San Diego Maritime Museum San
Diego, CA
World's oldest seafaring vessel
www.sdmaritime.com

72. HALLS OF FAME
Hockey Hall of Fame
Toronto, ON
www.hhof.com

Rock and Roll Hall of Fame
Cleveland, OH
www.rockhall.com

National Inventors Hall of Fame
Akron, OH
www.invent.org

Cockroach Hall of Fame
Plano, TX
Cockroaches dressed in costumes!
www.pestshop.com

The Texas Cowboy Hall of Fame
Fort Worth, TX
www.texascowboyhalloffame.com

National Cowgirl Museum and Hall of Fame
Fort Worth, TX
www.cowgirl.net

73. ARTISTS' INSPIRATIONS
Cedar Grove, the Thomas Cole Home
Catskill, NY
See the views that inspired the Hudson Valley
School of painters, the major American painters of
the nineteenth century
www.thomascole.org

N.C. Wyeth House and Studio and the
Kuerner Farm
Chadds Ford, PA
The farmhouse and fields where the famously
talented Wyeth family of painters and
illustrators worked
www.brandywinemuseum.org/kuerner.html

Grant Wood Studio
Cedar Rapids, IA
Studio of Midwestern painter, famous for
American Gothic
www.grantwoodstudio.org

Taos Art Colony
Taos, NM
Around the turn of the twentieth century, artists
began moving to this area, inspired by the desert
landscape
http://taoswebb.com/art

Emily Carr House
Victoria, BC
Home of the famous author and artist
www.emilycarr.com

74. UNUSUAL ANIMAL FARMS

Tupelo Buffalo Park and Zoo
Tupelo, MS
Largest buffalo herds east of the Mississippi River,
plus other animals
www.tupelobuffalopark.com

The Kangaroo Conservation Center Dawsonville,
Georgia
www.kangaroocenter.com

Bilbrey Farms
Edwardsville, IL
Llamas, pygmy goats, emus, zebras, miniature don-
keys, and more
www.bilbreyfarms.com

Aspen Acres Reindeer
Farm
Beausejour, MB
www.aspenacres.ca

Schreiner Farms
Dallesport, WA
Wallaroos, elk, camels,
buffalo, emus, and
llamas
www.schreinerfarms.com

77. REPLICAS

Woodleigh Replicas
Burlington, PE
Replicas of lots of world landmarks
www.woodleighreplicas.com

Venetian gondolas
Providence, RI
www.gondolari.com

The Great American Pyramid
Memphis, TN
www.emporis.com/en/wm/bu/?id=125479

Stonehenge, University of
Missouri-Rolla
Rolla, MO
www.legendsofamerica.com/
MO-RollaStonehenge.html

Viking ship and Norwegian stave
church, Heritage Hjemkomst
Center
Moorhead, MN
www.hjemkomst-center.com

Forbidden Gardens and Emperor Qin's terra-cotta
army
Katy, TX
www.forbiddengardens.com

Eiffel Tower
Paris, TX

Paris Las Vegas Hotel and Casino
Las Vegas, NV

Shakespeare's Globe Theatre
Odessa, TX
www.globesw.org

Stonehenge, Maryhill Museum
Goldendale, WA
www.maryhillmuseum.org

78. INVENTIVE PLACES

Alexander Graham Bell National Historic Site
Baddeck, NS
Home of the inventor of the telephone
www.pc.gc.ca/lhn-nhs/ns/grahambell/

Edison Labs
West Orange, NJ
Laboratory, library, and inventions of the famed
inventor
www.nps.gov/edis

US Patent and Trademark Musuem
Alexandria, Virginia
www.uspto.gov/web/offices/ac/ahrpa/opa/museum

Kitty Hawk, NC
Site of the first airplane flight; claims to be the
birthplace of aviation
www.nps.gov/wrbr

George Washington
Carver National
Monument
Diamond, MO
Birthplace of the famous
inventor
www.nps.gov/gwca

Jefferson County Pioneer Museum
Rigby, ID
Hometown and museum exhibit of Philo Farnsworth,
inventor of the television
www.blacksmithinn.com/museum.html

81. PLACES WHERE THEY MAKE COOL STUFF
Ben & Jerry's Ice Cream
Waterbury, VT

Snyder's of Hanover (pretzels)
Hanover, PA

The Crayola Factory
Easton, PA

The Hershey Company (chocolate)
Hershey, PA

Louisville Slugger Museum (baseball bats)
Louisville, KY

MoonPie Factory
Chattanooga, TN

Lionel Trains
Chesterfield, MI

Kellogg's Cereal City USA
Battle Creek, MI

General Mills Cereal Adventures
Mall of America
Bloomington Hills, MN

Mary Kay Cosmetics
Dallas, TX

Mrs. Grossman's Stickers
Petaluma, CA

Golden Gate Fortune Cookie Factory
San Francisco, CA

Boeing Corporation (airplanes)
Everett, WA

Prior Snowboards
Whistler, BC

83. LEGENDARY LOCATIONS
Tombstone, AZ
Scene of the famous shoot-out
at the OK Corral
www.ok-corral.com

Sleepy Hollow Cemetery
Sleepy Hollow, NY
Setting for *The Legend of
Sleepy Hollow*
www.sleepyhollowcemetery.org

Old South Meeting House
Boston, MA
Where the Boston Tea Party was organized
www.oldsouthmeetinghouse.org

Fort Raleigh
Manteo, NC
Near the original "Lost Colony" of Sir Walter Raleigh
www.nps.gov/fora

The Alamo
San Antonio, TX
Scene of the legendary battle of the Texas
Revolution
www.thealamo.org

86. CANYONS OR GORGES

Genesee Gorge, Letchworth
State Park
Castile, NY
"The Grand Canyon of
the East"
www.letchworthpark.com

Cloudland Canyon
Near Lafayette, GA
"The Grand Canyon of
the South"
http://gastateparks.org

Agawa Canyon (accessible only by train)
Near Sault Ste. Marie, ON
www.agawacanyontourtrain.com

Palo Duro Canyon State Park
Near Amarillo, TX
"The Grand Canyon of Texas"
www.tpwd.state.tx.us/spdest/findadest/parks/
palo_duro

Grand Canyon National Park
Near Flagstaff and Williams, AZ
www.nps.gov/grca

Columbia River Gorge National Scenic Area
Hood River, OR
www.fs.fed.us/r6/columbia/forest

87. MEDICAL MUSEUMS

Museum of Health Care
Kingston, ON
www.museumofhealthcare.ca

Mütter Museum
Philadelphia, PA
Anatomical oddities, medical instruments like brain
slicers, and human skulls with horns
www.collphyphil.org

Pasteur & Galt Apothecary Shop
Colonial Williamsburg
Williamsburg, VA
Eighteenth-century apothecary
shop
www.history.org/Almanack/places/
hb/hbpast.cfm

Country Doctor Museum
Bailey, NC
Nineteenth-century apothecary and medical instruments
www.countrydoctormuseum.org

Centers for Disease Control Museum
Atlanta, GA
History of global health
www.cdc.gov/global

New Orleans Pharmacy Museum
New Orleans, LA
Traditional and voodoo cures
www.pharmacymuseum.org

Indiana Medical History Museum
Indianapolis, IN
Old pathology center with operating theater, labs,
and anatomical museum
www.imhm.org/general.htm

88. AIRPLANE HANGARS AND COLLECTIONS

Canada Aviation Museum
Ottawa, ON
www.aviation.technomuses.ca

National Air and Space Museum's Udvar-Hazy
Center, Washington, DC
Historic aircraft and space shuttle in hangar
www.nasm.si.edu/museum/udvarhazy

National Museum of Naval Aviation
Pensacola, FL
www.naval-air.org/joinus/museum-history.htm

Hangar One
Glenview, IL
Museum in an old naval air station
www.hangarone.org

Tillamook Air Museum
World War II blimp hangar described as "the largest
free-span wood structure in the world"
Tillamook, OR
www.tillamookair.com

Museum of Flight
Seattle, Washington
www.museumofflight.org

89. PRISON AND JAILS
– Kingston Penitentiary/ Correctional Service of Canada Museum, Kingston, ON
– Old New-Gate Prison and Copper Mine, East Granby, CT
– Eastern State Penitentiary Historic Site, Philadelphia, PA
– Andersonville National Historic Site, Andersonville, GA
– Old Jail Museum, Montgomery County, IN
– Texas Prison Museum, Huntsville, TX
– Wyoming Territorial Prison Museum, Laramie, WY
– Old Prison Museum, Deer Lodge, MT
– Alcatraz, San Francisco, CA

90. HEROES' HOMES
Susan B. Anthony House, Rochester, NY
Civil rights leader who fought for women's right to vote
www.susanbanthonyhouse.org

Martin Luther King Jr. National Historic Site
Atlanta, GA
Childhood home and museum dedicated to the legendary civil rights leader
www.nps.gov/malu

Lincoln Boyhood National Memorial
Lincoln City, IN
Home of the president who led the nation through the Civil War
www.nps.gov/libo

Amelia Earhart Birthplace Museum
Atchison, KS
Home of the famous aviatrix
www.ameliaearhartmuseum.org

National Chavez Center
Keene, CA
Final resting place of the civil rights activist who fought for the rights of Latino farmworkers
http://chavezfoundation.org

92. FAMOUS ROADS
Toronto
Yonge Street (the "world's longest street" and "the most famous street in Canada")

New York
Wall Street (financial center of the United States)
Broadway (center of American theater)
Fifth Avenue (famous for prestigious stores)

Washington, DC
The Washington Mall (museums, leads to U.S. capitol building)

Beale Street, Memphis, TN (birthplace of rock 'n' roll)

Route 66 from Chicago to Los Angeles (former road through the rural West; called "the mother Road"; possibly the most famous road in U.S. history)

Extraterrestrial Highway, Warm Springs to Ash Springs, NV (site of many UFO sightings)

Los Angeles, CA
Sunset Strip, Sunset Boulevard (famous for celebrity watching)

Hollywood Boulevard (home to the Hollywood Walk of Fame)

Mullholland Drive (famous views; home of the Hollywood sign)

Rodeo Drive (famous expensive shopping)

94. AMAZING SCIENCE SITES
Thomas Jefferson National Accelerator Facility
Newport News, VA
Atomic and subatomic research
www.jlab.org, search tours

Ames Laboratory, Ames, IA
Technology research in applied mathematics, chemical and biological sciences, and condensed matter physics
www.external.ameslab.gov/final/Visitor/tours.htm

Fermi National Accelerator Laboratory, Batavia, IL
Study of neutrinos, the tiniest unit of matter in the universe
www.fnal.gov/pub/visiting/tours/index.html

Los Alamos National Laboratory
Los Alamos, NM
www.lanl.gov

Lawrence Berkeley National Laboratory
Berkeley, CA
www.lbl.gov

95. ECCENTRIC EATERIES
- Medieval Times, Toronto, ON (jousting while you eat)
- Medieval Manor, Boston, MA (castle)
- Mars 2112, New York City, NY (take a "translunar wormhole" to a Martian colony and eat in a cavern)
- South of the Border, Dillon, SC (major roadside attraction on I-95)
- The Pirate Houses' House, Savannah, GA (pirate theme in a real pirate location)
- Lambert's Café, Ozark, MO (they throw hot rolls at you)
- Safe House Restaurant, Milwaukee, WI (secret password at the door, spy theme)
- The Fort, Morrison, CO (replica of 1833 fort, recipes from frontier cookbooks and diaries)
- Casa Bonita, Lakewood, CO (25-foot waterfall, cliff divers, mine shaft, mock gunfights)
- The Mayan Restaurant, Sandy, UT (Mayan temples, cliff divers)
- Tail o' the Pup, West Hollywood, CA (hot dog stand shaped like a hot dog)
- Randy's Donuts, Inglewood, CA (donut stand shaped like a donut)

- Typhoon Restaurant, Santa Monica, CA (serves fried bugs)

97. WEATHER SPOTS
Brookhaven National Laboratory
Upton, NY
Laboratory that works on weather issues (among others), open to the public on summer Sundays
www.bnl.gov, search tours

National Hurricane Center
Miami, FL
Tours available outside of hurricane season
www.nhc.noaa.gov/aboutvisitor.shtml

National Severe Storms Laboratory
Norman, OK
Tours available by appointment
www.nssl.noaa.gov/faq/tours.shtml

My Notes:

About the Author

Joanne O'Sullivan is a writer and former educational travel planner who has lived and worked on three continents and traveled to over 20 countries. She's now settled in Asheville, North Carolina with her husband and daughter.

Acknowledgments

What a great adventure it was learning all about the wonders of this continent while researching this book! Thanks to Joe Rhatigan for the opportunity and the support. Thanks also to Rosemary Kast, Marthe Le Van, Rick Morris, Rose McLarney, and Michelle Elise for their research assistance and Susan Kieffer, Dawn Dillingham, and Karen Levy for fact-checking and editorial assistance. Thanks to Celia Naranjo and Robin Gregory for their time, effort, and wonderful design sense, and Bradley Norris for his assistance. And thanks to all the many photographers who contributed images to the book. Last, but certainly not least, thank you to Andrew for his support while I worked on this project, and to Maeve for letting me finish "just one more thing" again and again.

Photo Credits

Photo Credits (continued)

Page 42: ©Ingram Publishing
Page 43: (top right) ©iStockphoto.com/Peter Llewellyn; (bottom left) ©iStockphoto.com/Paul Senyszyn; (bottom right) ©iStockphoto.com/Robert Thesing
Page 44: (top to bottom) ©iStockphoto.com/Franky Sze, ©iStockphoto.com/Loic Bernard; ©iStockphoto.com/David Coder
Page 45: ©iStockphoto.com/Maartje van Caspel
Page 46: (top to bottom) ©2006 Jupiter Images Corporation; ©image100
Page 47: Jorge Vismara, with permission of the Niki de Saint Phalle Foundation
Page 48: (top and bottom right) ©iStockphoto.com/John Sigler; (bottom left) ©2006 Jupiter Images Corporation
Page 49: (top) ©iStockphoto.com/TK Edens; (bottom left) ©iStockphoto.com/Steve Simzer; (center) ©iStockphoto.com/Nancy Tripp; (right) courtesy of the National Park Service
Page 50: ©Anderson Ross/Getty Images
Page 51: ©iStockphoto.com/John Upchurch
Page 52: (bottom left) Frank Jensen; (bottom right) ©iStockphoto.com/seldomsee
Page 53: (top) ©iStockphoto.com/Sandy Jones; (center) ©iStockphoto.com/Gary Goldberg; (bottom) ©iStockphoto.com/David Freund
Page 54: ©Anderson Ross/Getty Images
Page 55: Bobbi Lane
Page 56: Victoria Garagliano/©Hearst Castle©/California State Parks
Page 57: ©Photodisc
Page 58: courtesy of Cypress Valley Canopy Tours
Page 59: (bottom left) courtesy of California State Parks

Page 60: ©iStockphoto.com/Brent Hatcher
Page 61: (clockwise, from left) ©iStockphoto.com/Rodolfo Arpia; Buddy Mays; William Springsteen
Page 62: ©2006 Jupiter Images Corporation
Page 63: ©Dynamic Graphics Group/Creatas/Alamy
Page 64: ©Medio Images/Getty Images
Page 65: (top) photo by Erika Sidor, courtesy of Old Sturbridge Village; (bottom) photo by Thomas Neill, courtesy of Old Sturbridge Village
Page 66: (top) ©iStockphoto.com/Arlene Gee; (left) ©iStockphoto.com/Nancy Louie; (right) ©iStockphoto.com/Johnny Lye
Page 67: ©iStockphoto.com/Tony Tremblay
Page 68: ©America 24-7/Getty Images
Page 69: (left)Michael Gassman/www.catsup bottle.com; (right) ©David R. Frazier Photolibrary, Inc./Alamy
Page 70: ©iStockphoto.com/Barbara Tripp
Page 71: (left) ©iStockphoto.com/Jim Jurica; (right) ©iStockphoto.com/Richard Stouffer
Page 72: ©iStockphoto.com/Pauline Vos
Page 73: Miro Vrlik
Page 74: (right) courtesy of Seattle Parks and Recreation
Page 76: ©Robert Miller
Page 77: ©CORBIS; ©Photodisc
Page 78: (top) David Turnley/CORBIS; (bottom) O. Rotem/Lebrecht
Page 79: Kim Sohee
Page 80: Cheryl Ridge
Page 81: ©iStockphoto.com/Bryan Delodder
Page 83: ©iStockphoto.com/Krzysztof Nieciecki
Page 84: (top) Milo Stewart Jr./National Baseball Hall of Fame Library, Cooperstown, New York; (bottom) ©Brand X Pictures
Page 86: ©iStockphoto.com/Clive Green

Page 89: (clockwise, from left) ©iStockphoto.com/Photos by Laurie; courtesy of the U.S. Air Force; iStockphoto.com/Vidar Thorlaksson
Page 90: Ron Saari
Page 91: (left) ©iStockphoto.com/William Walsh; (right) ©iStockphoto.com/Randy Mayes
Page 92: Rolf Hicker, Rainbow Productions
Page 93: ©Mark Joseph/Getty Images
Page 94: (clockwise, from left) Tom Craig, Directphoto.org/Alamy; ©iStockphoto.com/Pilar Echeverria; ©iStockphoto.com/Greg Nicholas
Page 95: Ron Niubrugge/wildnatureimages.com
Page 96: ©Digital Vision
Page 98: ©iStockphoto.com/Kevin Maude
Page 99: courtesy of The Colonial Williamsburg Foundation
Page 100: James Kirkikis
Page 101: ©iStockphoto.com/Rosica Daskalova
Page 102: ©iStockphoto.com/Mummu Media
Page 103: (top) ©Digital Vision; (bottom) ©iStockphoto.com/Nancy Louie
Page 104: (bottom) ©iStockphoto.com/Terry J Alcorn
Page 106: Peter Ginter, courtesy of Fermilab
Page 107: (top and bottom) Jeffrey Sward
Page 109: (top) courtesy of the National Oceanic and Atmospheric Administration
Page 110: ©2006 Jupiter Images Corporation
Page 111: ©iStockphoto.com/Lidian Neeleman
Page 115: (top left) ©iStockphoto.com/Brian Douglass; (bottom left) ©iStockphoto.com/Dan Bannister; (bottom right) ©iStockphoto.com/Bill Grove
Page 116: (top left) ©iStockphoto.com/Randall Chet; (bottom left) ©iStockphoto.com/Richard

Gunion; (bottom right) courtesy of the City of Hidalgo, Texas
Page 117: Layne Miller
Page 118: (top) ©iStockphoto.com/Andrea Gingerich; (bottom) ©iStockphoto.com/Jaleen Grove
Page 119: courtesy of the National Park Service
Page 120: (top) ©iStockphoto.com/Alastair Johns; (bottom) courtesy of the National Park Service
Page 121: (left)©iStockphoto.com/Danny Pfeiffer; (right) courtesy of the Dr. Seuss National Memorial Sculpture Garden
Page 122: all photos courtesy of the National Park Service
Page 123: (left) Royalty-Free/CORBIS; (right) ©iStockphoto.com/Christina Craft
Page 125: (left) ©iStockphoto.com/CJ McKendry; (top right) ©iStockphoto.com/Paiwei Wei; (bottom right) courtesy of the National Park Service
Page 126: (left) David Yanciw; (right) courtesy of the National Park Service
Page 127: (left) ©iStockphoto.com/Jim Jurica; (right)©iStockphoto.com/Peter Hibberd
Page 128: courtesy of the National Park Service
Page 129: ©iStockphoto.com/Bob Nixon
Page 130: (left) ©iStockphoto.com/Charles Beauchemin; (right) ©2006 Cary Ulrich/World of Stock
Page 131: (left) courtesy of the National Park Service; (right) ©iStockphoto.com/Wouter van Caspel
Page 132: (top) Joe Braun Photography; (bottom) courtesy of the Colonial Williamsburg Foundation
Page 133: (left) ©iStockphoto.com/Mark Hammon; (right) ©iStockphoto.com/Jan Bily
Page 134: Grant Goodge